DISCOVERING ANOTHER DIMENSION

Imagine looking into the eyes of an alien being and realizing that everything you thought you knew about yourself—your heritage, where you came from, who you *really* are—was a lie. That's exactly what happened to teacher, counselor and public servant Jim Walden when he looked up one night and saw an alien being standing at the foot of his bed. The events that followed would turn his world upside down and force him to rethink everything, from relationships to his concept of the universal order.

His story—rich with images of a secret underground testing facility . . . alien beings here on earth, operating within a fourth dimension . . . ancient religious figures revealed as aliens . . . the unveiling of an age-old human-alien hybrid program—sounds like the makings of great science fiction. But for Jim Walden, who had never had any interest in science fiction *or* extraterrestrials, these events were far from fictitious. Discover the details of what happened that night in 1992, and the numerous encounters that followed during his interdimensional search for the truth of his existence.

ABOUT THE AUTHOR

James L. Walden, Ed.D. (Pennsylvania), holds a doctorate in business education. He served as the city administrator of Eureka Springs, Arkansas, and has been a tenured associate professor of business administration. He participated in the development of the 12-part TV series *From Beyond*. This is his first book.

TO WRITE TO THE AUTHOR

If you wish to contact the author or would like more information about this book, please write to the author in care of Llewellyn Worldwide and we will forward your request. Both the author and publisher appreciate hearing from you and learning of your enjoyment of this book and how it has helped you. Llewellyn Worldwide cannot guarantee that every letter written to the author can be answered, but all will be forwarded. Please write to:

James L. Walden
℅ Llewellyn Worldwide
P.O. Box 64383, Dept. K779-X
St. Paul, MN 55164-0383, U.S.A.

Please enclose a self-addressed stamped envelope for reply, or $1.00 to cover costs. If outside U.S.A., enclose international postal reply coupon.

THE RE-ENGINEERING OF HUMANKIND

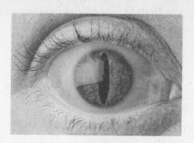

THE ULTIMATE ALIEN AGENDA

JAMES L. WALDEN, Ed.D.

1998
Llewellyn Publications
St. Paul, Minnesota 55164-0383

FIRST EDITION
First Printing, 1998

Cover design: Tom Grewe
Book design and project management: Michael Maupin
Editing: Rose Brandt

Library of Congress Cataloging-in-Publication Data
Walden, James L., 1946 –
 The ultimate alien agenda : the re-engineering of humankind/
James L. Walden. — 1st ed.
  p. cm.
 ISBN 1-56718-779-X (pbk.)
 1. Walden, James L., 1946- . 2. Alien abduction—United
 States   I. Title.
BF2050.W35 1998
001.942—dc21   98-13916
             CIP

Llewellyn Publications
A Division of Llewellyn Worldwide, Ltd.
P.O. Box 64383, Dept. K779-X
St. Paul, MN 55164-0383, U.S.A.

Printed in the United States of America

For loving, supportive friends
who listened without judging:
Jacquie Froelich
Barbara Harmony
Mary Henry, and
Erik Arnesen;
and for *Barbara Bartholic*,
whose tireless, selfless compassion saved my life.

CONTENTS

FOREWORD

During DECEMBER of 1977, a handsome, beguiling dark-haired professor politely declined an invitation to attend the premier opening of the epic UFO film, *Close Encounters of the Third Kind*. Dr. Jim Walden decided to spend the evening in his cozy study grading students' final exams.

The captivated audience that watched the Spielberg film that snowy night was unaware of the real-life UFO drama that was occurring simultaneously in their own neighborhoods, and throughout Arkansas.

Shortly after 7:00 P.M., the telephone lines at radio station KTHS in Berryville, Arkansas, were jammed with incoming calls as people tried frantically to report UFO sightings. Terrified teenage boys were chased home by a UFO that hovered over their car. A frantic mother claimed that her frightened daughter had been electrocuted by her curling iron as a UFO passed over their house. Farmers reported that their livestock went "ballistic," and ferocious guard dogs cowered in hiding as mysterious objects maneuvered silently across acres and acres of icy pastureland. Dismayed law enforcement agencies confirmed the event, and officers watched in awe while strange lights remained suspended in the dark winter sky. Personnel at the radio station received a tip that a "big one" was heading in their direction. Anxious announcers rushed outside just in time to watch an object, reportedly the size of a football field, glide slowly over the station building. During the following months, witnesses, ranging from nurses to nuclear scientists, continued to report the evening's unusual events. More than 200 people in Northwest Arkansas witnessed UFOs that December evening. Outraged farmers, nervous and deeply concerned about increasing cattle mutilations, formed heavily armed patrols. They camped in fields throughout long, eerie winter nights and were prepared to shoot the perpetrators if necessary, be they human or extraterrestrials.

My investigations of the unprecedented UFO encounters in Arkansas consumed nearly three years of my life and set the stage for my lifelong devotion to identifying and researching alien life forms that interface with humankind.

Fond memories of that time, nearly fifteen years earlier, flushed through my senses when I answered Dr. Jim Walden's introductory telephone call. He introduced himself in a soft-spoken, gentle voice. The thoughtful realist, and once-skeptical critic of alien encounters, spoke in a guarded fashion, trying desperately to avoid sounding insane as he described the recent disarming appearances of alien beings in his historic Victorian home. He cautiously told me about his abduction to an underground alien facility, described inexplicable marks on his body, and expressed his overwhelming fears of short, slender aliens.

When I responded to Dr. Walden's plea for help in understanding his contacts with alien beings and accepted his case, neither of us realized the significance or the magnitude of our future alliance. As his life's story unfolded, I learned that he had been a successful business manager and a respected educator at major universities in Arkansas, Missouri, and Oklahoma. A year before we met, he had accepted a leadership role in the management of Eureka Springs, Arkansas, a thriving resort community nestled in the grandeur of the primordial Ozark Mountains and known as "The Little Switzerland of America." Dr. Walden's demeanor suggested that he was in control of the alien intrusions in his life; but beneath his controlled facade, I perceived a man who was struggling to maintain one foot in the human world while the other one explored an alien dimension.

Throughout his unimaginable and traumatic encounters with aliens, Dr. Walden continued to execute his challenging duties as a city administrator with composure, dignity, and courage. Always considerate of other people, he was careful to avoid creating a fearful environment in a community where he, and many other residents, were being examined and manipulated by invasive beings from another world. UFOs and aliens returned to Northwest Arkansas during the spring of 1992. Cattle were spared; but the aliens targeted "human livestock" this time.

Investigations of human contacts with alien beings are time-consuming and complex activities. Hypnotic regressions are just one component of the total process of documenting and assessing such extraordinary events. The researcher and the subject must develop a continuous and integrated partnership, which may span several years or a lifetime. Both must be dedicated to an unending quest for understanding relationships between humans and aliens; and the researcher must be committed to providing tireless support, counsel, and comfort to the subject. As Dr.

Walden's case illustrates, such researchers evolve with their subjects. The investigations of his accounts of traumatic alien abductions have facilitated the development of new theories about the presence of alien beings and their interactions with humankind.

You either believe in this phenomenon or you don't. For most people, belief is experientially based. For those who experience the alien presence, naive concepts of human reality are forever shattered. Dr. Jim Walden was a researcher's dream. For nearly five years, he meticulously documented the extraordinary events of his life with pristine accuracy. He was valiant in his efforts to acquire understanding of his alien abductors. Dr. Walden stepped across the boundary that separates human consciousness from human-alien connections and returned with greater understanding of himself, humanity, and interdimensional worlds.

Barbara Bartholic
Tulsa, Oklahoma
June, 1998

Part One

1 | THE NIGHT MY LIFE CHANGED FOREVER

I WISH I could forget the alien who stepped through my bedroom door and abducted me from my home. In an instant, this experience transformed my life, and forced me to question every one of my core beliefs.

It all started one night in March 1992. I had enjoyed a pleasant evening at home, and got to bed at the usual time. In bed, I read for a few minutes until I felt ready to fall asleep. My bedroom wasn't completely dark; street lights shone into the room through six large windows. It was just as I dimmed my bedside lamp that the alien stepped through my bedroom door and glided to the foot of my bed. Simultaneously, cold air filled the room. I was wide awake, but petrified with fear and terror. I began to cry.

The alien stood at the foot of the bed, its large dark eyes focused on me. The memory will always be engraved in my mind. The being was between four and five feet tall, with a bulbous head, disproportionately large for its thin, frail body. Its gray skin appeared cool, moist, and leathery. As I looked into its face, all its features disappeared, as if it were becoming invisible. I strained harder, but now could only see its silhouette.

Then, the being's right eye enlarged and turned bright red, as if activated by the flip of a switch. A brilliant beam of red light streamed from it and penetrated my right leg, just below the knee—where I felt a sudden stinging pain. I jumped up in bed and grabbed my leg with both hands. I was chilled, confused, sobbing, and terrified. I said out loud, "I must be dreaming!"

I was so terrified of the alien that I couldn't bear to think about it—so I told myself that a spider must have bitten my leg. I jumped from the bed and ran into the bathroom. I stood there for a few minutes, paralyzed with fear, repeating that it was "just a spider bite." When I was finally able to move, I found some ointment in the medicine cabinet and rubbed it on the small, red spot on my leg. I didn't think about the alien. Transfixed by the red spot on my leg, I just kept repeating to myself, "A spider bit my leg. A spider bit my leg." In a few minutes, I began to feel drowsy, and an inner voice told me to return to the bedroom.

As I fell onto the bed, I felt drugged, but still aware of my surroundings. The alien returned—this time, simply appearing at the foot of the bed. My only reaction was to sob loudly in terror. Again, I felt chilled. Although warm spring air was flowing through the open windows, I was shivering. Eventually, sheer desperation gave me a burst of energy; I leaped off the bed and back into the bathroom.

I slumped against the bathroom wall. My leg no longer hurt, but my eyelids felt very heavy. I struggled to overcome the drowsiness and remain conscious. I knew that the being was still waiting for me. "You can't hide in the bathroom forever," I told myself.

As if in response to my thoughts, a powerful telepathic voice commanded me to return to the bedroom. As I walked, my legs felt like soft rubber, and could hardly support my weight. Just outside the bathroom door, I fell into an antique rocking chair. Struggling to stay awake, I wrapped my arms tightly around my chest and clenched my legs together. The rocking and the sound of the creaky old chair reassured me that I was still alive.

"Are you trying to kill me?" I asked.

In response, I heard another telepathic command to return to the bed. Although I couldn't resist the voice, I couldn't walk, either. As I left the chair, I tumbled to the floor, and remained there for some time before I could muster the strength to crawl to the bed. I was still sobbing loudly; I was mentally, physically, and emotionally exhausted—but I couldn't defy the being's commands. As I dragged my heavy body onto the bed, I felt numb—as if anesthetized.

As soon as I rolled onto the bed, the alien directed its chilling energy at me; my body temperature dropped, and I started shivering again. "This is its third attempt to freeze me," I said aloud, trying to force my brain to function.

By this time, however, I was helpless. Just as I was losing awareness of my body, I saw a beam of white light above me, moving slowly and steadily toward me, as if my gaze was locked with something approaching in slow motion. My eyes were still focused on the light beam as it entered my body, just below the navel. As the beam of white light penetrated my body, the voice said, "Relax. Do not struggle."

I exhaled deeply and released my resistance, and a floating sensation came over me. My physical body was nearly frozen, and my mind was withdrawing into unconsciousness. My last thought was, "The being is taking my life."

When I came to, I was lying on my back on a hard, cold table, with a surface like polished metal. I was immobilized—I couldn't move any of my limbs. When I tried to focus my eyes, I could only blink in pain; a bright overhead light was shining right into my face. I was surrounded by beings in stiff white smocks, peering clinically down at me.

The beings were observing me and examining my body. Some of their faces appeared to be human, but most of them looked like the alien being who had stood at the foot of my bed, except that their eyes were not red and enlarged.

Although I couldn't see beyond the faces and the bright overhead light, I sensed that the room was quite large. I seemed to be in a sterilized area, and I wondered if it was a surgical room.

My mind seemed to be functioning again, and I estimated that as many as a hundred beings were present. When I tried to focus on their faces, their features dissolved, and I could only see transparent silhouettes. I was helpless to do anything but lie there in the bright light.

My memories of this experience are somewhat fragmented. I remember that the beings touched and examined every part of my body, and were particularly interested in my groin. I remember feeling humiliated when they extracted a sperm sample.

When the examination was over, I heard the telepathic voice again. I don't remember all that it said, but I will never forget what I do recall.

As I heard the words, images appeared in my mind, like a movie. "You are in an underground facility located beneath southeast Kansas," the voice said—and I saw that far above the facility was a flat wheat field in new growth.

At the edge of the field, a steep hill rose, covered by leafless trees that were just starting to bud.

The voice said, "You are participating in a peaceful, cooperative experiment." I remembered that I had seen a mixed company of experimenters—both human and non-human. "You will not be harmed," it added.

I also remembered that some of the humans had small glowing red objects implanted underneath their right middle fingernails. I now realized telepathically that these were monitoring devices. In response to my unspoken question, the telepathic voice said, "These human workers are volunteers who are learning to control human disease."

I didn't believe this. I couldn't understand why humans would volunteer to work cooperatively with alien beings. *They're captives*, I thought.

I wondered why I had been brought to this facility. The telepathic voice responded, "We're interested in working with you because of your ability to send and receive information." I interpreted this as a reference to my psychic abilities—and suddenly regretted my twenty years of work as a psychic counselor.

The telepathic voice continued, but by now I was incapable of absorbing any more information. I only remember one more thought: "You are not who you think you are, and you must accept this!"

2 | SLEEP IS IMPOSSIBLE

THE NEXT thing I knew, I was back in my own warm, comfortable bed. I scanned my bedroom, searching out all its familiar shapes and shadows. A faint reflection in my bedroom mirror assured me that I really was home in bed again. I was so glad that I caressed my quilt and hugged my pillow. "Yes," I thought, "I'm really home."

Curiously, I didn't feel disturbed, or in shock—just blissful and sleepy. I rolled onto my left side, my favorite sleeping position, and fell asleep. (Had the alien scientists given me an anesthetic?)

The next morning, however, was anything but blissful. My emotions erupted with volcanic force—images of alien beings and the underground examining room surged through my mind. I felt drugged. I just wanted to cry and cry...as if tears could wash away the terrifying memories. I knew that my mind, my body, and my being had been violated. I was terrified by the alien intruder's total power over me. "When they're finished with me, they'll kill me," I said aloud to myself.

During the following days, I was an emotional wreck. I cried continuously, and the memories of the aliens and their underground facility ran through my mind uncontrollably, in a continuous loop. Occasionally, a vivid new detail would work its way into my awareness. I had to struggle to force the terrible memories from my thoughts during the day, so I could work at the office.

Restful sleep was impossible. Before it was invaded by the alien, my spacious bedroom had been my favorite room. Afterward, I was afraid to be in there at all. The image of the alien's glowing red eye haunted me constantly; I could no longer relax, or enjoy any activity. I withdrew from my friends and lost weight. I felt fatigued and depressed, victimized and helpless.

I could not escape the awful memories. All my fragile rationalizations failed. "An alien being abducted me!" I thought repeatedly. Rather than forgetting, I gradually remembered more and more—and my memories of this experience initiated a life-long interdimensional search for the truth.

Before March 1992, I had zero interest in aliens, UFOs, or science fiction. I had an outright aversion to science fiction books, TV programs, and movies. A persistent friend talked me into going to *Close Encounters of the Third Kind*. When I finally saw it, I just dismissed it as a silly movie. It never occurred to me that any of it might be based on reality, or that anyone else might have really encountered an alien. To me, aliens were science fiction fantasies—and this was one reason my own alien encounter was so disturbing.

So, while remembering more, I was also trying to deny that the encounter had ever happened, and this complicated my recovery. I was filled with unresolvable mental and emotional conflicts. For months, suicide loomed in my mind as the only acceptable solution. I continuously questioned my sanity, and sometimes wondered if the aliens had programmed me to destroy myself. In a way, I was destroyed already—when the intruder entered my bedroom, my old life abruptly ended, and for a long time I thought that life would never again be worth living.

I could no longer sleep in my bedroom. Although logic told me that the alien could have entered any of the thirteen rooms of my large Victorian house, I felt safer sleeping elsewhere. Most often, I ended up making my bed on the dining room floor. A street lamp stood directly in front of its large windows—and I told myself that alien beings wouldn't dare enter such a brightly lit room.

One night, the downstairs guest bedroom seemed like a good alternative but sleep wouldn't come. I was lying on my back and searching the ceiling for sleep, when I heard a loud "whishing" sound. Something moved toward me at lightning speed—and a large, life-like image of George Washington stopped right in front of my face, touching my nose. I heard a loud, forceful voice say, "George Washington was one of us. So are you. You must accept!"

At the time, I didn't understand this cryptic message. It had no more meaning to me than the previous statement that I must accept a new definition of myself. I asked naively, "Was the father of our country an alien?"

Perhaps I should have entered my early encounters in a journal, but I didn't expect to live long enough to complete one. For a while, I lost hope that anything good would ever happen to me again, and my negative thinking nearly destroyed me.

As the weeks passed, however, I slowly began to recover some of my physical and emotional strength. I alternated between long, painful episodes of feeling like a victim, and sudden, brief bursts of determination to understand what had happened to me. I began to accept the inexplicable emotional roller coaster that my life had become.

Then, early in June, something wonderful happened. As I walked into my office one sunny morning, the receptionist called and said, "Two women are waiting in the hall. They want to interview you."

As I walked down the hall toward the two women, I felt particularly drawn to one of them—a redheaded woman, sitting on a bench. She seemed disturbed, and didn't speak when I introduced myself. The other woman, who was standing, smiled and moved toward me as I approached.

She said her name was Rachel, and she was researching a book about ghosts. She wanted to verify some ghost stories about a Victorian hotel that I'd managed some twenty years before—she'd found my name in the hotel records. "Did you meet any ghosts while you worked and lived there?" she asked.

Captivated by her enthusiasm, I spoke freely about my encounters with the hotel's unseen residents. After thanking me for my stories, she lowered her voice and added, "In addition to these interviews, and reviewing historical documents, I'm also trying to identify some of the ghosts through psychic research."

The quiet woman hadn't taken part in our conversation—her head was turned toward the door. Now, Rachel glanced at her and said, "Jane is a gifted psychic. I asked her to tour the hotel and report her psychic impressions about the alleged spirit entities."

I was drawn to Jane, and found myself staring at her delicate, attractive face. Her red hair was aglow in the morning sunlight. I felt compelled to speak to her. Abruptly, I turned to her and asked, "Jane, did you rest well last night?"

Although it was an unusual question to ask a stranger, I expected her to respond in some way. Instead, her eyelids moved up and down, but she didn't answer or make eye contact. She just adjusted her position on the bench, and continued to gaze through the glass door panels.

Rachel stepped in and said calmly, "Jane thinks that an alien molested her last night."

"At the hotel?"

"Yes," Rachel continued. "She's disturbed because an alien being entered her room during the night and sexually molested her."

Something clicked inside me. Finally, another person who had encountered an alien being! And she, too, was very disturbed. I wanted to hear more about her experience; I wanted to know if our stories matched up. Until that moment, it had never occurred to me that any others might have been contacted by the alien beings. Now I felt some comfort. *If Jane has encountered an alien being*, I thought, *I may not be insane, after all*.

Rachel closed her notebook, saying that they were ready to leave town—and a sense of urgency swelled in me. I had to talk to Jane, and I knew I had to act quickly. I felt a mental connection with her, and I had to know about her alien encounter.

I turned to Jane and said, "You must be anxious to get on the road. May I walk to your car with you? I'd really like to hear about the alien being who entered your hotel room last night."

Rachel smiled and excused herself, saying, "I'd like to buy some postcards, Jane. I'll meet you at the car in a few minutes."

Jane and I left the building together and stepped into the lovely spring morning. The car was nearby, so I said quickly, "I was abducted by an alien being several weeks ago, and I've been very disturbed. I didn't know that anyone else had been visited."

"I was first abducted by alien beings seven years ago," Jane replied. I could tell that the memory was still painful to her. I discovered that she was a veteran of many alien encounters; her original contacts with the aliens had disturbed her deeply. Tears welled in her eyes as she confided, "When it happened, I admitted myself to a mental institution. I really thought I was insane." Jane's anguish was expressed in words and tears; her sincerity touched my heart.

She pointed to the nape of her neck. "Aliens implant programming devices in humans for various purposes. They use these devices to control and communicate with us." After speaking frankly about her alien encounters, she assured me, "You aren't insane." Her story gave me hope for my own survival.

Reaching to open the car door, Jane hesitated. She turned to me and said, "I know someone who might be able to help you. With your permission, I'll ask her if she'd be willing to counsel you about your alien encounters."

"That would be wonderful!" I replied. I wrote down my phone number and handed it to her. "Please call me collect and let me know if your friend would be willing to talk with me."

Three or four days passed, and I didn't give much thought to our conversation. When Jane called early one morning, I was surprised but it was great to hear her caring voice. "Jim," she said, "I talked to my friend, and she's very interested in your recent encounters with aliens. She's an alien-abduction researcher."

I couldn't disguise my surprise. "A researcher?"

"Yes," Jane replied. "One of the best."

Panic rushed through me. I had never considered talking to a researcher.

"Here's her phone number," Jane said. "She's expecting you to call."

I wrote the number down and thanked Jane for her help. Then I sat quietly for several minutes, trying to decide whether to call Barbara Bartholic, alien-abduction researcher.

3 | THE REGRESSION BEGINS

ALTHOUGH I was reluctant to tell my story to a researcher, by now I was too desperate to care. As the disturbing encounters continued to torment me, my life hit bottom—I was sick, frightened, and lonely.

As I picked up the phone to dial Barbara Bartholic's number, I didn't know what to expect. While the phone rang, my sense of apprehension grew. I felt as if I was about to share my most intimate secrets with a stranger. Barbara's comforting voice soon put me at ease; she seemed to understand how the alien beings had shattered my life. Within minutes, I decided that I could trust her. I tried to visualize her face, and wondered what she was like in person.

Except for a few details, Barbara already knew my story—she had heard the same story hundreds of times from other clients. After first easing my sense of anxiety and pain, she began asking me some routine questions to verify that I had had a genuine alien abduction. Within a few minutes, I was ready to tell her everything—and soon I felt as if I had shared my heart, my soul, and my secrets with her.

Afterward, I heard her pause and exhale deeply—and then, with a sense of deep compassion, she said, "I think you've had legitimate encounters with alien beings. If you need my help, I'm here for you anytime."

Now, the alien intrusions began occurring almost every day; I became afraid to be home alone. The encounters often happened around three o'clock in the morning, and they left me feeling drugged, unable to move. My limbs seemed disconnected from my brain; terrified, I would struggle helplessly to simply move a leg or an arm to the edge of the bed. To focus my mind and regain awareness, I began to time my recovery periods. One typical Sunday morning, forty-five minutes passed before I could reach for the telephone.

During those weeks, I called Barbara almost every day. She was always there for me, and her calming voice was able to pull me back into physical reality. I became dependent on her—she was my anchor and my lifeline. She was the only person who knew about my encounters so far. I couldn't tell my relatives, and although some of my friends might have listened politely to my stories, I knew I wouldn't enjoy the jokes that would follow.

Barbara emphasized the importance of talking about my encounters. She also recorded each call, explaining, "Your reports may provide information that is helpful to others." Only after several weeks of patient listening did she suggest that hypnotic regression might help me understand the experiences—"when you are strong enough to learn more."

The idea of being hypnotized was intimidating. I didn't want to relive my alien encounters; I doubted that I had the emotional strength to handle it. However, by the end of June, I was suicidal, struggling for survival—and I knew the time had arrived to take drastic action. Barbara invited me to visit her over the three-day Fourth of July weekend.

As I turned west on the highway toward Barbara's house, I felt nervous and lonely. I was thinking that this Fourth of July would sure be different from my powerful childhood memories of family Fourth of July celebrations on the Kings River. I could still smell the fried chicken and taste the sweet watermelon. Now, my life lay in ruins, and I was filled with anxiety about reliving the alien encounters under hypnosis.

When Barbara stepped out of the house to greet me, my surprise was obvious; my preconceived image of her could not have been more wrong. I had imagined her as a stereotypical researcher—slight build, little if any makeup, plain clothing and glasses. Instead, I was hugged warmly by a tall, blonde, beautiful woman with a flair for fashion. She ushered me inside and made me feel right at home. When I asked about the paintings and sculptures that filled the living room, I learned that Barbara and her husband, Tim, were both artists.

As Barbara explained her research, the phone rang constantly, and I noticed that she counseled each caller with the same caring tones that had comforted me. It was clear that she was working with many abductees. "Each person is important," she said. "Each abductee is another piece of the gigantic alien-abduction puzzle."

Barbara encouraged me to talk freely about my experiences, but avoided expressing any of her own beliefs—she said she didn't want to influence me or plant ideas in my mind. But she did say, reassuringly, "I believe you"—and later she added, "I think I know what really happened to you, but I can't say it yet." We discussed my experiences for several hours before she finally asked, "Would you like to look at your alien encounters under hypnosis?"

Barbara arranged a pallet of pillows and cushions for me to stretch out on; as I lay down, the crackling sound of fireworks filled the room. It seemed that the country was celebrating its independence—and I was about to discover mine. While Barbara fussed with the tape recorder, the video camera, and the lights, I had plenty of time to release my anxieties about hypnosis.

Barbara turned on some celestial music, and soon even the loudest of the fireworks explosions were absorbed into its harmonies. Barbara's relaxation suggestions were familiar to me, and I soon drifted into a relaxed and peaceful state. Under the influence of her soothing reminders, I forgot my fears; my mind slowly gave in to her soft, hypnotic voice. I placed my trust completely in her—my last conscious thought was, "She'll protect me while I'm under hypnosis."

I was lying on my back with my arms at my sides, deeply relaxed, when something amazing happened. A slender gray alien being—just like the first one I had seen—suddenly emerged from my body. Still attached to my lower body, it sat up quickly and looked startled. It seemed to be trying to understand what was happening and where it was. After a moment's hesitation, it turned its bulbous head from side to side and surveyed the room. Then it stood upright and, in one springing motion, leapt into the air and disappeared through a closed window. Turning to Barbara, I said, "That's what they put into my body, isn't it?"

"What, from your understanding, was put into your body?" Barbara asked, as she calmly engaged the recorder.

"A being," I replied. "They made it possible for an alien to inhabit my body. But I didn't know that it had been inside me until just now."

"The being has left your body," Barbara assured me. "How do you feel?"

I snapped, "Foolish!"

Barbara looked into my eyes and asked, "Why do you feel that way?"

For a moment I couldn't respond; my vocal cords felt swollen. Finally, I replied, "I should have known that the alien was inside me."

At the time, I didn't understand the being's abrupt departure, or the significance of my remark. But the image of the being living inside me remained vivid in my mind, and disturbed me more than any of my other encounters. For nearly two years afterward, I would wonder if the alien had returned to my body.

Barbara now proceeded with the regression; her voice soon carried me into a dreamlike state. I was dimly aware of my surroundings, and occasionally heard distant-sounding bursts of fireworks, but mostly I was relieved to be free of the burdens of my awareness. Following Barbara's hypnotic suggestions, my pallet of cushions turned into a fluffy white cloud. Her reassuring voice knew the way, and I was ready to follow it deep into my subconscious.

"Do you want to talk about anything specific?" she asked.

"I see nothing."

"Take yourself back to the night when the alien with the bright red eye appeared at the foot of your bed."

"I see an entire face!"

Under hypnosis, I could see the alien's face clearly for the first time. The top of its head was rounded and large in proportion to its narrow, pointy chin. Its most prominent features were large, dark, slanted eyes. As I watched, the right eye enlarged and a beam of glowing red light moved toward me. "Did the red light control my mind or body?" I asked.

Barbara asked me to describe the alien's face further, but I couldn't see any ears, nose, or mouth. "Please, Jim, look carefully at the alien and tell me more about it."

I told her that I could sense that its soft, leathery skin was cool and moist. "And when it entered my bedroom, I smelled a foul, musty odor, which I had never smelled before. My fear of it was like my fear of poisonous snakes."

Barbara encouraged me to look at the being more closely. "Can you say more?"

My response surprised both of us. "I don't have to be frightened now," I said calmly. "The voice in the laboratory was right. I am one of them! I don't need to be fearful; I simply need to remember who I am."

4 | GOING DEEPER

As I tried to sort through the confused thoughts that filled my mind, Barbara suggested, "You are floating in space. Your mind will take you, your soul, and your consciousness to the most important memories you need to recall in this session. You can go to any point in time. You can travel in time anywhere you wish. Take yourself back, now."

Going deeper into the hypnotic trance was like entering an enormous library, in which all my memories were carefully bound and shelved. As Barbara guided me deeper and deeper, I began to select memories from the shelves of my subconscious library, and watch them come to life.

Barbara now said, "Take yourself to the night when you looked into the alien's large, glowing red eye."

The alien who invaded my bedroom again came into focus—but this time, in more detail than ever before. "There's an area right here," I said, pointing to my forehead, "where I was programmed to be helpful to other people. The aliens have many different human programs, and I received 'intuitionist' programming, which allows me to look into other people's minds."

23

Barbara asked how I received the programming.

"I see a glass tube…and I'm in it!"

With those words, forty-five years of beliefs of myself vanished. As the image of a human embryo in a glass tube became clearer, I understood for the first time why the alien had said that I wasn't who I thought I was. The image forced me to consider that my life might have begun in an alien laboratory, rather than a human womb.

My hypnotized mind said that I had been part of a group of experimental human embryos—and I began to hear the thoughts of the alien scientists who had created me. "They were concerned about my development," I said. "My embryo was a challenge; it almost died—or it did die, and they had to resuscitate it."

As scenes of my creation appeared before me, I watched the alien scientists discussing my embryo; they weren't sure it was useable. "They almost disposed of me because I wasn't developing properly," I said sadly.

The alien scientists appeared to be compassionate beings. "They didn't destroy me, even though they were concerned about the success of their experiment. They must have felt some kind of emotional attachment. They were gentle and caring."

Barbara asked me to view the scene again and report all details of my creation.

"I started out in a glass tube, and then my embryo was brought into this dimension and implanted into my mother's womb. My human parents weren't my real parents. My mother never knew about the alien implantation that resulted in my birth. They went to her while she was sleeping, anesthetized and opened her, inserted a tube, and pushed me into her body."

As I described this discovery, disturbing thoughts flooded my mind. I remembered an evening twenty years earlier, when my mother and I had discussed my budding psychic abilities. She had confessed to me, "I don't know why—but when you were born, I knew that you were different from other children. I raised you differently, and allowed you more freedom."

My mother was right. All my life, I'd felt different from my siblings and peers. Under hypnosis, I could see my life from a new perspective, and pieces of my life's puzzle began to fall into place. I thought vividly, "I was right! I've been right all along! There *is* more to life than I learned from religion and education."

By accepting the existence of aliens, I had opened myself to ideas about human evolution that felt absolutely right to me. "Interdimensional alien beings are directing the evolution of humankind!" I said. It occurred to me that Baby Louise wasn't the first test-tube baby. Alien scientists had probably created millions of test-tube humans long before.

After discovering that I was a test-tube baby, I was filled with questions. I drifted away from Barbara's voice and began a probing discussion with myself. I looked into my mental mirror, searching for a familiar image of myself—but it had disappeared. All traces of "myself" had been replaced by something unrecognizable. I felt fragmented and helpless.

"Let's continue. Look at one year of age," I heard Barbara say, trying to reach me.

"I don't like physical life; it's a struggle," I said, close to tears. At that age, I wasn't comfortable with human thoughts and feelings, and did not remember that I was more comfortable—more "at home"—in another dimension.

"Why were you created?" Barbara asked.

"I'm confused! I've just been in a head-on collision—my forty-five years of human life have just collided with seeing my embryo in an alien test tube."

Barbara guided me to a deeper state, and said calmly, "Please tell me more about your creation."

"In the tube, I was given special brain cells. I am a composite of other people and beings. Some parts of me came from humans; others came from aliens. I'm not unique. I am composed of parts of all the people who were used to create me!"

I saw the alien beings harvesting brain cells from dying human bodies, then combining the cells to make my embryo. Barbara asked how the aliens had extracted the brain cells. I said, "I see the corpses of two men and one woman. When they died, the aliens—who cannot be seen by humans—are present, and they retrieve tissue samples to use in creating me." As I realized that I was part human and part alien, the word "hybrid" came to mind.

The woman's corpse was the most vivid. I didn't recognize her, but I was aware that she had a superior intellect. "I'm not an individual," I repeated.

I hesitated, trying to accept that I was a composite of three people and other aliens. I was angry, feeling that the interdimensionals had robbed the people of their biological cells and ethereal essences. "Do aliens take the best features of the donors?" I wondered indignantly.

"Let's hope so. Do you know any of the donors?"

I didn't think so; but something about them was familiar, and I wondered if they had had intuitive abilities. "Maybe I'm the next link in an evolutionary chain of intuitive hybrids—maybe I'm an improved version of them."

When Barbara asked me to tell her how I felt at one year of age, excruciating pain suddenly filled my head, as if invisible forces were striking at me. I grabbed my head with both hands and tried to protect myself from the invisible blows. "I don't like being a child! I want to be older." I wanted to say more, but I couldn't talk because of the pain.

"Was your head injured when you were a child?" Barbara asked.

"Maybe when I was born."

Barbara assumed that I was re-experiencing my birth, and suggested that I "slip over to the other side," and imagine being in the womb.

I responded, "Actually, the side of my head may have been hit by something before I was born."

Barbara tried to stimulate my memories about the origin of my head and jaw pain. Then she suggested that I look inside my head at the time my jaw was first affected. Immediately, I knew what had caused the pain.

"A tiny object was placed in my head!"

I described the unknown object as "a small BB-sized thing." As I thought about it, I massaged my jaw, my left temple, and the base of my skull. The pain was so unbearable that my head felt like it would explode.

"The object isn't made of metal—and when I was about six months old, my head was hit again." As I remembered Jane's comments about the implant in her head, I felt comfortable saying, "The aliens forced an implant through my ear and into my head. It was an organic substance that functioned as a communication device."

"Did this occur while you were in the womb, or after you were born?"

"I'm not sure what happened in the womb; but I know that something was implanted in my head when I was about six months old. Before that, the aliens weren't sure I would live, and they didn't want to waste time on me. The implant was used to monitor my progress and to communicate with me, or control me."

Barbara encouraged me to speak about the implants, but I didn't know where to begin. My mind was filled with images of aliens; the journey into my subconscious was turning out to be as traumatic as the trip to the underground laboratory. I realized that my life had been a series of encounters with alien beings, and that I was probably just one of their millions of hybrids. "Humans have improved horses, cattle, and dogs," I reasoned, "and alien scientists are improving us, in the same way. But we have foolishly assumed that we occupy the top rung of the intelligence ladder."

Barbara didn't ask another question right away. When I became aware of the silence, I said, "The Earth may actually be an alien-controlled human experimentation farm."

Barbara knew I was burdened with disturbing thoughts, and she gave me the suggestion to rest for a few moments.

After resting I said, "I'm six now." I was still in hypnosis, and one of my carefully guarded secrets was struggling for release. I was reliving a traumatic childhood experience in which "Judy," a babysitter, had raped me. For years, I had suppressed the memory of the rape—and the feelings of being embarrassed, dirty, guilty, and fearful that had resulted. I was afraid that my parents would discover what had happened, and blame me. So it's not surprising that I didn't remember the actual experience of being raped.

Now, however, I vividly relived the experience of being raped in a bedroom closet by an overweight adolescent girl. My hands felt the disarrayed clothing on the floor; the metal clothing hangers on the floor pressed into my bare back. I relived the traumatic moment when the babysitter unzipped my pants, while holding her hand over my mouth. The impact of her heavy body terrified, and nearly crushed, me. Then I heard the approaching footsteps of her mother, and my heart raced. Her mother asked in her usual voice, "Where are you kids?" I didn't want her to find us or to be angry with me for doing something bad.

Barbara asked me to breathe deeply and relax. "It wasn't her fault! I didn't know what to do. I was afraid, so she held her hand over my mouth. I don't know why they made her do it!"

I hesitated, trying to comprehend the words that had just gushed from my mouth. "We were being watched. They wanted to know if my programs were working properly. I did not want to be with her!"

"Be in the experience and look around," Barbara instructed calmly. "You said that the rape wasn't Judy's fault. Who was there?"

"Until now, I didn't know anything about this," I replied, "and I'm having difficulty with it." I felt like a small child confessing to a scornful parent.

Barbara suggested that I place my confusion in a drawer and close it. I followed her advice and was able to look at the rape scene again. This time, I saw images that my mind had suppressed for nearly forty years.

"They came through the walls! They came through the walls!" I shouted, as frightening scenes flashed in my mind. "Aliens watched us," I said tearfully.

"How many beings were present? How many watched?" Barbara asked.

"First three, then four, then six…they were invisible at first; and I didn't see them."

"Did Judy see the beings?"

"No, I don't think so—but her mother must have known that something was happening. She must have looked into the bedroom; I heard her heavy footsteps hesitating near the closet door. I didn't want her to open the door."

My anxiety mounted. "Judy was manipulated…it was an experiment…the aliens wanted to see if I could function," I said indignantly.

Barbara asked why the experiment was conducted. I told her that the aliens were testing my sexual abilities.

"Did you pass the test?"

"I survived. I'm still alive."

Barbara asked how the recurring pain in my jaw related to the rape.

"Fear, maybe. I couldn't yell for help. I was afraid to tell anyone, so I kept it a secret for nearly forty years."

Barbara guided me back to the rape scene to look at it more closely.

"The aliens were disappointed in me. They didn't like it. Judy forced me to do something bad, and her size and strength frightened me."

"Did they want you to be more sexually stimulated than you were?"

In response, I relived Judy's hot, heavy body rolling off me. I immediately reached for my clothes and tried to cover myself. I focused on a stream of light gushing through an open crack in the closet door—it was my link to freedom and safety, but it also stimulated my feelings of guilt and dirtiness. "The aliens discussed me telepathically, but I was too upset to understand their thoughts."

"Observe carefully. Try to understand what they were thinking."

"They were deciding whether to let me live or to dispose of me." I felt disappointed in myself. "The aliens were displeased with my sexual performance."

Barbara asked me to explain this. "I was developed to accelerate the aliens' experiments. They expected me to be sexually capable early in life, earlier than normal humans."

"Why did they want you to be sexually capable at such a young age?"

"They were trying to develop a group of human hybrids whose sexuality would develop early. These advanced sexual and reproductive abilities would allow the aliens to complete more human life-cycle experiments in less time."

"You were six years old! Did the aliens really expect you to have sexual intercourse with Judy?"

"I think so. I didn't perform according to their schedule. They wanted me to be sexually advanced, but I was progressing like a normal human. They weren't pleased with my inability to complete the sexual act." I sighed deeply. "The aliens used Judy to test me; they controlled her thoughts and actions."

Barbara asked how the pain in my head was related to the rape. I said, "When they forced the implant into my body, it hurt—and my fear of Judy and of the aliens was emotionally painful."

"Why was your sexuality so important to the aliens? Why not your intellect?"

"The aliens said there is a link between the development of my testicles and my brain. They expected my brain to take a big leap when my body experienced puberty, when my testicles were activated."

Suddenly, I began screaming, "You've got to take it out! They put a new one in my ear! Help me get it out! It hurts!"

Barbara told me to put the pain in my head in a place where I couldn't feel it. Then, she told me to rest. When I was calm again, she asked, "Why did you feel pain?"

"Some time after being raped, I was playing in a cow pen by myself; the spring grass was tall, nearly to my waist. I was walking near a fence when the aliens appeared, and one of them looked like Judy at first. They stunned me, and again forced something into my ear." As before, I felt excruciating pain as I recalled the encounter. "They were trying to charge my brain."

I held my head and tried to confine the pain. When I was able to speak, I thanked Barbara for helping me. I was not only discovering the truth about my encounters with alien beings, but also about forty-five years of self-doubt and fear. Amidst all the physical and emotional pain, I felt comforted.

The intense pain of reliving the second implant caused me to come out of my hypnotic state. My mind was wild with questions about aliens. I said, "I want to understand them. I want to ask them why they do these things to people."

Barbara looked at me sympathetically. "Please, Barbara, tell me how alien beings can glide through walls, abduct people, and create human life in a glass tube." Beneath my emotions, I heard a calm and distant voice say, "Your human logic will not prevail when you seek answers about us."

Like other telepathic messages I had received from the aliens, I didn't understand this at the time. I didn't grasp the fragility of human logic in relation to alien intelligence. I asked bitterly, "What if the aliens are using us as experimental subjects, the way human scientists use rats and mice?" I felt victimized, and couldn't find any positive rationalization for the aliens' behavior. I resented their control over human lives.

"The aliens may answer these questions later," Barbara said, while reinstating my hypnotic trance. She was now ready to explore my abduction and my experience in the underground laboratory.

Under hypnosis, memories of the encounter were lucid and readily accessible. Since it had been difficult to process my sensory perceptions in the alien dimension, at first I just noticed a lot of descriptive details that I had not remembered earlier.

"I was naked and restrained. I could see aliens and humans and hear some of their thoughts and mental conversations. My fingertips felt the polished surface of the examination table, and the room was cool and damp."

Barbara asked how the beings had extracted my semen. I said that I didn't understand the alien technology and gave her a long, tearful explanation of their semen-extraction procedure. "Energy came toward me, and when it entered my stomach, semen was released. They wanted my body to produce sperm for them. I felt humiliated. They treated me like a research animal."

Barbara repeated the question.

I said, "The energy, or light, penetrated my body. When it entered my stomach, maybe below my navel, it caused me to release semen. Afterwards, I couldn't feel sexual. I didn't have any interest in sex for a couple of months afterward."

"Did you feel yourself ejaculate?"

"No. I didn't have a physical reaction or release. It was more like a milking process."

I was distraught, and did not want to relive this humiliating experience; but I nevertheless followed Barbara's suggestion to describe it more fully.

"I was naked; many faces were peering down at me. My legs were spread apart and restrained. I couldn't move my limbs. They invaded the most private area of my body, and depleted my dignity. I thought they were going to castrate me. They treated me the way humans treat animals when they neuter them."

By now, I was nearly hysterical. "Barbara, are they finished with me? Will I be of further value to them?"

"You're very important," Barbara said. But as I relived those frightening moments, I didn't feel important. She encouraged me to look deeper into the details of the experience. "How were you positioned when the semen sample was extracted?"

I couldn't control my hypnotized mind. It was determined to answer Barbara's questions quickly and honestly. I was often surprised when thoughts that I'd never heard before leapt from my mouth. This time, I said, "My human body was at home in bed!"

This was startling, and at first I fumbled for words. Then I said, with many pauses, "I told you how the alien chilled my body and lowered my vibrations. While my human body was chilled, my other body was transported—the aliens took the rest of me away. I'm aware of two bodies. One is human, and it's on my bed in my house. However, I can feel the legs of my other body as the aliens pull them apart. This body is on their examination table, and they are applying pressure between my testicles and anus. It hurts! I don't understand how I can have these feelings when my human body isn't present. The aliens are not gentle. They're hurting me."

When I agreed to the regression, it never occurred to me that I would be discussing such intimate topics with Barbara. She was aware of my embarrassment, but spurred me to go deeper, asking, "What was the purpose of the pressure?"

"To prepare my body to release semen."

"How did they apply the pressure?"

"When they were ready, a very bright light was directed toward me. The light caused my semen to ooze out. My muscles had been anesthetized, and the light caused a free-flowing drainage that didn't require any physical or mental stimulation. Do they still want me to live?"

"Yes! You are valuable to them. Was your body paralyzed while you were on the table? Could you resist them?"

I pointed to the implant behind my ear and said, "It's like placing metal on a magnet. The aliens can block my thoughts and control my mind. If they don't want me to speak certain information, for example, they'll send a signal to the implant, and my mind won't able to process the thought. They can manipulate my body, as well."

"The aliens block your mind by activating the implant?"

"Yes."

"Bypass it!" she demanded. "Go down and get the memory of what happened to you, now! Focus on the alien facility and your other body. Describe the body that's restrained on the table."

"When I'm out of my human body, I look like them!"

We were both shocked. Barbara inhaled deeply before asking, "When you were on the examination table, you were in an alien body?"

"Yes. I looked like the aliens."

I don't know what Barbara was thinking, but my thoughts were, *Please, Barbara, don't think I'm insane.* Although I couldn't believe it myself, I desperately wanted her to believe me. But I had to confess, "I don't know if I can accept this. As the regression began, I saw an alien leave my human body—an alien that looked just like the body on the examination table. I don't understand how this is possible."

Barbara didn't waver from her search for answers. "How did they use your semen? What was their purpose?"

"You already know the answers," I said, squirming. I couldn't avoid the questions, but I wanted to avoid the ensuing discussion.

"Please, tell me."

"I do not want to talk about this!" I shouted. Fear swelled my throat. Under hypnosis, I was realizing something that correlated with some conscious memory fragments I had reported to Barbara weeks before.

"Please."

"My fears may come true," I sobbed.

I knew what I was about to see, but I couldn't block it. Dreamlike encounters drifted in my mind's eye, and the memory fragments came alive. My semen had been implanted in a human woman—the aliens had used my sperm to create a human embryo!

"Please tell me what you know about the destination of your semen."

I felt angry and humiliated. "To the aliens, it's just ongoing research. They're trying to evolve humans to their level of intelligence. I don't understand why they're doing this."

"What do you know about the woman who received your semen?"

"Barbara, I don't want to live. I'm ready to die."

She must have known that I was getting tired; I'd been in hypnosis for more than four hours. She said, "Jim, you're discovering a new world—you must learn how you and other people are being affected by the aliens."

I snapped, "You don't understand! I'll never be like other people."

Barbara assured me that she did understand, and I knew that she was right. The information I was discovering about alien beings was changing my conception of human life. Barbara counted me down to a deep, restful place, and then said, "Tell me how your semen was used."

"The woman's from the same stock. We're from the same inventory." I raised my right hand and drew hiero-glyphic-looking symbols in the air. "That's it. That's the designation for our inventory. The aliens wanted to mate two hybrids from the same strain; they used my sperm to test our compatibility. The experiment was as insignificant to them as a veterinarian inseminating a cow to produce a better calf."

"Is she carrying the fetus now?"

"No. I think the aliens removed the embryo from her womb later. I don't know what the aliens did with it." I added, "This woman has been used as a human incubator more than once."

I vowed that I would not allow the aliens to use me for their human engineering experiments anymore, but quickly realized my helplessness and conceded, "I can't do anything to stop them."

"Look at this carefully," Barbara said. "Do you know this woman? Have you had any physical contact with her? Have the aliens manipulated you two in any other ways?"

"I don't recognize the woman, or remember any physical contact with her. But later we were used for another phase of the experiment."

Barbara asked how I knew about the experiments, and I reminded her of the alien being who'd left my body early in the regression. I said, "After the aliens successfully inseminated the woman with my sperm, the next phase was to mate our interdimensional bodies."

"What do you mean?"

"They used us to test the possibility of human conception outside of physical bodies. The alien scientists brought our interdimensional bodies together to determine if conception could occur in their dimension—and the experiment was successful."

"What does that mean?"

My emotions swelled in my throat. "We produced a human-like child who is now being cared for by a surrogate mother in the alien dimension."

As I bounced from scene to scene, I felt like a Ping-Pong ball. Thinking of the child aroused my parental feelings; I felt a deep sense of loss for a child I'd never known.

Sensing my emotional distress, Barbara guided me deeper into my subconscious and changed the subject. "Let's go back to something else. The alien voice said that the underground facility is a peaceful, cooperative venture. Tell me more about this arrangement."

"Yes!" I shouted, with hysterical laughter. "The *humans* cooperate!"

"Are humans involved in the facility?"

"Oh, yes," I said scornfully. "They're there, and they're peaceful. They believe that they're involved in a peaceful, cooperative program; they don't know what's really happening."

Barbara wanted to know if there were any human military personnel in the facility.

"Not where I was examined. Only aliens and civilians." Then I added, "Well, I didn't see any military uniforms. Everyone was wearing white smocks."

"How would civilians be procured?"

"Volunteers, I assume. I can't imagine anything funnier than this. Those people feel like heroes, but they're ridiculous. I can't stop laughing at them. They think they're doing something important. I'm not that stupid. I didn't have a choice about being there; they did."

I wanted to cry, but continued to laugh, perhaps as a way of denying my fears. "They're silly gooses—they get some mind-controlling thoughts and believe that they're the first humans to work cooperatively with alien beings. If they only knew...."

"Did our government agree to this arrangement?"

"I think so. It's supposed to be a peaceful, cooperative venture, but the aliens are in control."

I felt a deep sadness. "The human volunteers have glowing red implants under their fingernails. When they leave their assigned areas, the implants transmit signals, and they're returned right away. They really are volunteers, aren't they?" I continued to laugh, as if I had just told the funniest story. Later, I told Barbara that I had enjoyed this part of the regression. But while laughing, I was also crying.

Barbara realized that I was traumatized by this discussion; she allowed me to laugh and cry until I calmed down. I guess I was laughing to avoid the pain of the experience.

I heard Barbara say, "You've done a wonderful job. Please rest now, rest and relax." She guided me out of the trance, and as I returned to the conscious world my first question was, "What time is it?" I couldn't hear the fireworks—but I assumed that I'd been out for maybe fifteen or twenty minutes.

"It's after two in the morning."

We had started the regression at 9:00 P.M. I asked her, "What have you been doing for nearly five hours?"

Barbara smiled. "Regressions are like surgical procedures. They require a lot of time. I've been right here beside you."

"Yes. I feel like I've had mental surgery." For sure, I had sliced an opening in the veil between the dimensions.

"I have a lot to learn about alien beings," I said. "There's so much more to see. I feel that tonight I've simply glimpsed the mountain peak from a distance. The aliens seem to show us only what they want us to see, and tell us only what they want us to hear."

"Before you can understand more, you must assimilate the information that we recorded tonight. You'll have to watch the videotape and give yourself time to understand what's happening in your life."

I promised to study the video, and thanked Barbara for her help. I was filled with hope, ready to live again. But I still needed to know why the aliens had invaded my life; I had to understand my relationship with them more deeply.

Barbara's last words were, "As I mentioned earlier, people usually feel quite different after their first regression."

5 | THE DAY AFTER

WHEN I awoke in Barbara's guest bedroom, the world seemed quiet and peaceful. Mid-morning sunshine filled the room; a gentle flow of fresh air caused the curtains to rise and fall, as if they were breathing. My mind was still clouded by deep sleep, and for a moment I didn't remember going to bed. Then I recalled Barbara saying, "Take this blanket. You may get cool out there."

As my brain finally came to life, I remembered that after the session Barbara and I had talked for two hours. How could we have gone to sleep after such a profound experience? As the fog lifted, I realized that I'd slept for nearly six hours.

Sleep had been a miraculous healer. Just six hours earlier, I'd been an emotional wreck. Now, for the first time in months, I felt peaceful and rested, happy to be alive. I realized how lucky I was to have Barbara's help. During our two-hour discussion after the regression, she had listened patiently while I vacillated between feeling enlightened and feeling victimized.

I heard voices, and assumed that Barbara and her husband were already up. I decided to be a thoughtful guest and allow them more time together before I made my appearance. Certainly, I had plenty to think about. As I rolled onto my side and placed my hands under my ear, memory flashes of an early morning dream caused me to bolt out of bed.

"Was it really a dream?" I wondered. The memories were more vivid than my usual dreams. But I didn't want to believe that aliens had visited Barbara's house that morning. "Did you remove an implant from my head?" I asked, as if I expected an answer from them. I touched my ear—it was painful. I noticed fresh blood stains on the pillow, and an image of a pearly object filled my mind's eye. Were the stains a calling card left by the alien visitors?

Imagine the sensation of having a piece of string pulled through your ear. The pearly object in my mind's eye was attached to a fine cord. *The aliens pulled the implant through my ear*, I thought to myself.

When I opened the living room door, Barbara was arranging her video camera and reviewing the regression tape. "You did a wonderful job last night," she said, as she glanced at my image on the screen. Breakfast was waiting, and Barbara was anxious to discuss the regression.

Seeing oneself on television can be startling, but seeing oneself on television under hypnosis is another matter entirely. As I ate breakfast, Barbara was scanning the tape for interesting segments. She was locating discussion topics for our post-regression interview. I don't remember what I ate; I was too distracted by the images flashing by on the television. Memories of the regression began to flow into my consciousness. I listened in awe as I heard myself make startling, strange statements.

After breakfast, Barbara asked me to sit in a sturdy handmade chair, while she tested the lighting and focused the video camera.

"As I said last night," she began, "people are usually in better condition when they leave. What were you feeling when you arrived yesterday?"

"I wondered if I was crazy, and those negative thoughts were taking a lot of energy out of me. I felt weary, and filled with disturbing ideas, feelings, and emotions. I was trying to figure out whether my encounters with aliens were real, and I truly believed that I might be losing control of my mind."

"And how do you feel this morning?"

"I'm happy this morning," I responded cheerfully. "I now believe that my contacts with alien beings are real. So I'm not insane! In fact, I suspect that many other people are having similar experiences."

Barbara smiled. "Do you have more control of your life now that you've gained some understanding of your alien encounters?"

"Oh, yes. Memories of the encounters were robbing me of physical and emotional strength. Although I slept only six hours, I feel rested this morning. I'm much more peaceful than yesterday. The regression restored some of my self-control, and hopefully, I'll heal myself."

Barbara didn't specifically explain the purpose of the post-regression interview, but I understood that she wished me to understand my alien encounters. Working with so many abductees, she knew the importance of reviewing and discussing the regression. I was grateful for the opportunity to discuss it; I wanted to reconcile my thoughts and emotions before I left.

"During the regression, you experienced a new reality, and you understand now that you're not crazy. You now see your contacts with alien beings as a part of your life experiences," Barbara summarized.

I nodded. I *had* glimpsed another reality. The regression had allowed me to access a new world. "My fear of the aliens has lessened, and I no longer feel as if they're trying to kill me. Also, I have insights into the alien dimension…and I can't explain how I acquired that information."

"Please, try to tell me what you mean."

"The hypnotic experience was like driving through a new community. You can glean general information by observing the people, the buildings, and the landscaping. After reliving my encounters under hypnosis, I understand that I've experienced an alien dimension—they took me there. Hypnosis allowed me to bring those suppressed memories into consciousness. But along with memories of my alien contacts, I also have a considerable general knowledge of their reality—and I must have acquired it while I was in their dimension."

"That's a very important observation," Barbara said. "How will it affect you?"

"I can't answer specifically. I can't understand all the implications now. But because of my knowledge of their reality, or dimension, I may be able to answer general questions about aliens."

Barbara smiled, and suggested, "Let's go to the beginning of the regression now. Remember, I took you to a mountain and asked you to look for numbers behind it. What were those numbers again?"

I had seen the number one in large, bold print, and also a second number, zero, which was not as obvious. However, during the regression, Barbara had encouraged me to explore the "zero" instead of the "one." She now explained that "zero" represented experiences that occurred before birth. "What happened when you went to the zero?" she now asked.

Barbara was referring to seeing my embryo in a glass cylinder, which I called a tube. She asked me to elaborate. "The tube was vertical. It was less than a foot tall, and about two or three inches in diameter." This tall, slender cylinder, filled with a fluid, was just large enough for a tiny human embryo.

Every detail was important to Barbara; now she wanted to know more about the fluid. "Do you remember what color the fluid was?" she pressed.

"It was transparent, but had a slight gold coloration."

She asked me to tell her about being in the tube.

"I can't remember being in the tube," I offered. My primary memories of this stage were thoughts about the beings who were creating me. "As I glimpsed myself in the glass cylinder, I was alarmed, because the aliens were deciding whether to destroy the embryo or to give it more time to develop."

Barbara was especially interested in the alien scientists who cared for the embryo. "You spoke of the scientists as caring beings. Can you explain this?"

After my frightening experiences with aliens, I had also been surprised by this comment. I wasn't sure what it meant, but I was convinced that they felt an emotional attachment. "The two scientists who cared for me seemed to be genuinely concerned about my development. They watched me vigilantly; once, I even saw them share their energies with the embryo, through their eyes. I believe that they assumed some risk in allowing a dubious embryo to develop."

"Most abductees do not describe alien abductors as caring beings," Barbara said, cautiously.

"Well, perhaps they were concerned about the success of their experiment, rather than my individual embryo."

"You saw what you now think was the creation of your life. How does this concept differ from your previous concepts?"

"Before this, I had studied metaphysics. I believed in reincarnation, and assumed that my soul had lived many lifetimes on Earth. I believed that humans were created by a Supreme Being. Now, I'll have to reevaluate all those beliefs. My metaphysical studies had always been haunted by the question, 'Where and when was my soul, or spirit, created?' Now I would say that I was manufactured."

As I said this, a sense of aloneness swept through me. I thought of my lifelong inability to feel close to my family—and the three human corpses came to mind. The idea that I had been created from the cells of other people was deeply disturbing. I wondered whether people who receive organ transplants have the same eerie feelings of discomfort.

Barbara suggested that I visualize the corpses again.

"I wish I'd observed them more closely under hypnosis," I said. "My images of the woman are the most vivid. She may have been in her seventies. The two men were middle-aged or older."

"Can you tell me anything else?"

"In addition to their biological cells, the aliens harvested their ethereal essences, too." As I strained to understand my own words, I added, "I wonder what else is in the recipe for a human-alien hybrid."

"Look again. What did the aliens extract from the corpses?"

"I only saw the donors' heads—and I assumed that something was extracted from their brains. During the regression, I rubbed my brow here because I felt that something was being removed from their brains. I suppose that could have been cells, fluids, or alien-implanted objects."

Changing the subject, Barbara asked, "What do you think caused the pain in your head?"

"I'm not sure. The pain occurred when I tried to answer some of your questions. At the time, I assumed that these questions involved topics that the aliens didn't want me to discuss."

"What are your thoughts about that this morning?"

"They could have been blocking information that would have been painful for me—or they may not be ready to reveal certain things." As I answered, my internal voice said, "The pain occurred because the aliens did not want you to reveal specific details yet."

Barbara mentioned the link I had reported between the pain and the implantation of alien devices in my head. She asked, "Do aliens really implant such devices in people? Remember, I asked you to use x-ray vision to learn more about them."

When she said this, I suddenly remembered something that I hadn't told her during the regression, I'm not sure why. Perhaps the aliens didn't want me to divulge certain details yet. "While I was a fetus, something probed my mother's womb." I first wondered whether this was a memory of my parents having intercourse, but as I thought about it, I realized that it was something else.

"While I was a fetus, I was hit on the side of the my head—imagine the force of a stapler or a BB gun. Something was implanted on the side of my head, and I experienced that kind of impact."

"When I asked you about this before, you saw a BB-sized object," Barbara reminded me.

I recalled a pearly object, and more oval than spherical. "It was made of an organic substance, not metal." It looked like a baroque pearl, strung on a strand of fine silk. "It was a living organism, with intelligence, or programming; and it moved around in my body. It was a communications device programmed to interact with the alien communication center."

"Do you remember anything else about the alien implants?"

"They may contain programming for various stages of physical, intellectual, and emotional maturation. The aliens may have changed the programming devices in my body several times."

Barbara asked whether I had suffered any serious diseases or health problems in infancy. I had to laugh, remembering all my parents' humorous stories about my sickly infancy. According to them, I was allergic to every form of nourishment. As a last resort, a wise old doctor prescribed fresh goat's milk, which saved my life. For several months, they had to take a goat with them everywhere they traveled. Although the goat ate through the cloth top of their car and pulled down their camping tent, it also kept me alive. Was this an example of a hybrid infant's struggle to adapt to human life?

Barbara chuckled at the goat stories and asked, "Did any other unusual events occur during your infancy?"

This reminded me of my childhood "close encounters" with reptiles. "My parents have a story of the time they found a large coachwhip snake coiled around me in my crib—and my mother still has the dried-out rattles of the rattlesnake that I befriended while a toddler."

Barbara asked me to tell her more about the rattlesnake.

"My mother was at the kitchen window, watching me play in the backyard. She thought I was playing with a thick rope, until she saw the "rope" begin to coil. Then she saw that I was holding a rattlesnake, just below its head. She rushed over, grabbed the snake and carried it to the chopping block by the woodpile, where she chopped its head off with a hatchet. She removed the rattles and has kept them in a jewelry box for nearly forty-five years…nine rattles and a button!"

Barbara asked if I had an affinity for reptiles.

"I'm fascinated by snakes," I said, as she twitched with repulsion. "I like to look at them, although I don't care to touch them. But I wonder if they aren't attracted to *me*. After all, I didn't go looking for the coachwhip—it got into our house and crawled into my crib."

At this point, I didn't know why Barbara was asking these questions, and I certainly didn't understand the implications of my responses.

Barbara now moved on to another topic. "Did you know about the rape before last night?"

"I often had painful memories about it during my youth. It was a haunting and depressing experience. I didn't want anyone to know about my encounter with her, because I felt like a sexual failure."

"Why did you need to keep it a secret?"

"The experience was very hurtful, but I may not have thought of it as 'rape' until last night. I guess I told myself that it was just sexual exploration between a six-year-old boy and an adolescent girl curious about male anatomy. When I was six, 'rape' was not in my vocabulary."

"Last night, however, you did consider it to be a rape?"

"Yes! I felt raped."

"When you learned that Judy wasn't totally responsible for her actions, how did you feel?"

"Shocked. I now believe that alien beings directed her to rape me. She was just a pawn in their experiments; they probably gave her telepathic commands. The rape was a test. They were checking to see if I was progressing on their accelerated sexual schedule. This is very disturbing."

Barbara asked, "Can you understand that many cases of child incest and rape—sexual child abuse—may be set up by aliens?"

This rang true. "Yes. Today, we would call what happened to me child abuse. But forty or fifty years ago, that wasn't a common term."

"Considering the current epidemic of child abuse, your case may provide new clues. According to recent statistics, one out of three girls and one out of five boys have been molested."

"Yes—I can see how child molestation may be correlated with the aliens' human-engineering experiments. After driving my new car for the recommended miles I take it in for a checkup and servicing. Likewise, when aliens create a new human, they have to check it out periodically, to determine if it is maturing on schedule. If not, they have to decide whether to scrap the project or make adjustments—and I barely escaped being scrapped!"

"During the regression, you reported feeling dirty afterward. In addition, you were afraid of Judy, her mother, your parents, and the aliens. Your fear and guilt led to a deep sense of trauma. Can you forgive Judy now for all the discomfort you've endured?"

Yes, I could forgive her for all the pain I'd felt—because I could see now that she had been manipulated, too. "I wonder if the emotional side effects were part of the overall program for my life. If they had developed me for hybrid breeding purposes, this may have been a way to prevent me from becoming sexually involved with women other than those they selected."

This intrigued Barbara. "Absolutely! Maybe this was their method of check and balance."

Barbara's enthusiasm was contagious. As the questions and answers flowed, new theories emerged. She was tireless in her search for information about the alien-abduction puzzle. "According to your understanding, the alien scientists gave your embryo an 'intuitionist' program. Can you tell me more about their human programs?"

I told her again that alien scientists have developed an array of human programs, or life orientations, which they use to create human hybrids. I was programmed to serve others; and most of my life has been devoted to service, as a public official, educator, and psychic counselor. "My life exemplifies one category of alien programming," I replied—but I was having trouble focusing on Barbara's question. I had suddenly remembered the alien being who had left my body. "Can we discuss what happened at the beginning of the regression?" I asked.

"Do you mean the alien who left your body?"

"Yes. I need to understand what happened."

"Please tell me your perceptions."

"You were still giving me relaxation suggestions; I was lying on my back, relaxed, but not yet fully hypnotized.

Then an alien being sprang up, removing itself from my body like a layer from an onion. Until that moment, it never occurred to me that an alien might be living in my body." I hesitated and inhaled deeply. "What are the implications of having an alien in my body?"

"That's a very important question. If an alien being is living in your body, are you totally responsible for your thoughts and actions?"

"Its influence could have been positive or negative. Since most of my life has been positive and productive, it may have been helpful; but it could have had negative influences, too."

I knew from the wrenching feeling in my gut that we were discussing something very significant. I said, "We're not interpreting this correctly!" But I could only perceive the alien as an external being or force, and I felt victimized—assuming that it had invaded my body.

I said, "I wonder about people who have multiple personalities or schizophrenia. Could they be hosting aliens? I'd like to shake some of them and see what leaves their bodies!"

Barbara moved on to the next topic. "Remember when I asked you what the aliens were going to do with your semen? You said that you were interdimensionally mated with a human woman. Have you ever thought about anything like this before now?"

"I never thought about contributing...."

Barbara completed my sentence. "You never thought you would be a sperm donor, did you?"

"No. I never thought of it."

"Yet the information came out clearly during the regression. Why was this revealed to you?"

"I don't know. I tried to avoid the topic, but I believe now that alien scientists used me to create life. They extracted my semen and used it to impregnate a woman. But the two of us may not have been the only contributors. I don't know if they altered the embryo, or if other biological or etheric ingredients were combined with it. "

I wandered into memories of the interdimensional mating. The aliens took my interdimensional body to a strange bedroom, and surrounded me as I floated over her sleeping body. A man was asleep, snoring, on the other side of the large bed. He didn't move. Although the woman was asleep, too, I could see her alien body floating above her human body.

"Barbara, how could the union of two interdimensional bodies result in the creation of life?" Before she could answer, however, I reminded myself that "human logic does not prevail in such matters."

Barbara replied, "I can't comprehend either the aliens' intelligence or their human-engineering technology."

In my mind's eye, I was standing on the bed, straddling the woman. My interdimensional senses were alert; I could see, hear, and feel. Alien hands began to touch me, stroking me sensually. I tried to resist, because I knew they were preparing me to penetrate her.

I heard a voice say, "She's ready to receive you now." Although the thought of violating a strange woman's body disturbed me greatly, I couldn't stop myself from drifting toward her. As my body approached hers in slow motion, my anxiety increased, but I was helpless to resist. As our bodies became entwined, I lost consciousness.

"Jim, what do you know about this? What's going on?"

I had drifted away, and hadn't heard Barbara ask about a new topic. "Can you be more specific?"

"The underground laboratory in Kansas."

Her question pulled me back into the interview. "The attitude was clinical. My first memories were of alien and human faces. Everyone was dressed in white, knee-length smocks. It may be a sperm-bank operation. My view from the examination table didn't allow me to see much. Also, I was restrained, and the bright overhead lighting blinded me whenever I tried to look up."

"Why was the facility developed?"

"I perceived it as a high-tech human-engineering laboratory. I think many kinds of human-alien hybrids are produced there." Piercing pains shot through my head. "I'm not under hypnosis now, am I?"

"Are you getting interference?"

"Penetrating pains in my head, just like I felt during regression...I can't concentrate. What were we talking about?"

"The white smocks. Did you see insignias or emblems on them?"

"No, but somewhere in the facility I saw an American flag." I started to laugh. "Do you know of a military base in Southeast Kansas?"

Barbara said she was aware of a large military base in Kansas. "But it may be farther north than the area you described."

I was now sure that a military operation was located near the subterranean facility. Stabbing pains again struck my head as I struggled to say, "The civilians think they're learning about human diseases." I grasped my head with both hands and tried to confine the pain. I had to stop talking for several minutes, and finally said, "I'm trying, but I just can't talk about the underground facility."

"How does the pain affect you?"

I responded slowly and deliberately. "It creates interference, and I may not be allowed to tell you much more about the alien facility. The humans think they're in a disease-control center—but the alien scientists have other objectives, which they're not sharing with the humans."

Barbara asked about the "other" objectives, and I said, "Human engineering is the primary objective. The aliens are creating various kinds of hybrid beings, who are part alien and part human."

The pain returned again. After recovering my ability to speak, I said, "I can't focus on this topic. We shouldn't talk about the underground facility."

But Barbara responded, "I demand to know why aliens are conducting human-engineering research! Why are they harvesting sperm from thousands of people? What are they doing with the embryos?"

"Do you really want me to answer your question? Do you really want to know what they do with the embryos?" I asked, close to tears.

"Yes! You say it, Jim. I already know."

I began to cry. Words formed, but they remained stuck in my vocal cords. I couldn't say them. "You never knew about this, did you?" Barbara asked, wiping a tear from her cheek.

I shook my head. I couldn't answer her. I just knew that some human embryos might be used as nourishment for aliens. I wondered where and when I had acquired this idea. Finally I said, "I must have seen or heard something in the underground facility about this."

"It is happening, isn't it, Jim? I'm sorry that you had to face this. Before our session last night, did you ever think that alien beings might consume human flesh?"

"No, and I'm angry with myself for being so damned stupid."

Barbara assured me that I shouldn't feel stupid. "In surgery, you don't feel the insertion of the surgeon's scalpel. You can't feel your appendix being removed from your body, because you are anesthetized—and during the encounters the aliens also anesthetized you. Until last night, you didn't know much of what has happened in your life. Don't blame yourself for not knowing."

"But I may have fed them."

"What?"

"My sperm may have been used to produce food for them. I don't know how to deal with this." I cried for several minutes.

"Will the atrocities ever end?" I asked, trying to speak again. My perception of life was bleak. "Why do we have to live like this? Why can't humans and aliens share this planet peacefully?"

"Of course we could. But then we wouldn't produce babies for their nourishment."

"You're right. Humans would never willingly submit to the aliens' needs; it would be incompatible with our respect for human life."

Neither of us wanted to speak about this topic; we sat silently, as our tears dried on our cheeks. "Life is evolution," I finally said. "The aliens should be able to adapt and learn to coexist with us." Then I remembered my earlier statement about the Earth as an experimental farm.

Barbara asked, "Jim, why were you allowed to see all this? Why did the aliens permit you to remember and divulge this information? Why?"

"I don't know." I had no plausible explanation. Although sad and disturbed, I also felt empathy for them. I wanted to find a way to justify their behavior. "Was their homeland destroyed? Are they doing what's necessary for their survival?" I searched my mind for understanding. "Is our planet at risk? Did the aliens come here to show us how to save our planet?"

The interview had been helpful, but tiring. I felt over-burdened, and confessed, "Barbara, I don't know whether these new thoughts are my own, or whether they're from the alien voice."

She pulled me back by saying, "You've done a wonderful job—again." We were less than four feet apart, but her reas-suring voice could have been emanating from a distant mountain peak. I was submerged in unfathomable thoughts of alien intruders.

I heard her say, "You know, it doesn't matter if just one person produces this kind of information. But when it comes from so many intelligent and educated people, the pieces form patterns; and the patterns can be used to develop new knowledge. I would like to discover more pos-itive patterns; but knowledge—positive or negative—is our only source of power."

As an afterthought, she added, "The aliens seem to be orchestrating your awakening."

"Yes. They're revealing information about their dimen-sion and their agenda to me. Sometimes I wonder if they're simply trying to perpetuate their species; other times, I think they're just trying to understand human life. I'm caught between these two possibilities, and I don't under-stand why. Oddly, I'm never truly angry with them."

"They must have reasons for allowing you to learn so much about them."

"You may be right. For one thing, they may trust me. Trust is the foundation of effective communication—and they may be grooming me for something that we don't know about yet." I wasn't sure I liked what I had just said, and quickly countered with: "Or, maybe I'm simply an alien-abduction survivor."

"Are you here to build bridges between us?" Barbara asked. "Is this why you're being awakened?"

I shrugged. "I don't know yet."

We could have gone on for hours, but the morning had already faded into afternoon. The weekend was ending much too quickly; I wasn't ready to say goodbye yet. For one thing, I felt safe in Barbara's home—and for another, she believed in my alien-abduction experiences.

The post-regression interview was helpful in many ways. My sense of being victimized became less intense, and I had a new perspective on my experiences. I wondered whether there was another part of me residing in some other dimension, and whether the conscious part of me ever visits that dimension. But these thoughts were ahead of schedule.

As we exchanged our goodbye hugs, I said, "Barbara, I'm beginning to think that part of me is more at home in another dimension. That's why I'm so disturbed after my encounters with aliens...I just don't want to return to the harsh reality of the human world."

6 | WRITING IT ALL DOWN

WILL I ever be able to convince people that an alien walked through my bedroom door?" I wondered aloud, as I turned at the end of Barbara's street and headed toward the highway.

The sound of my voice felt foolish, but talking to myself calmed the turbulence in my mind. My mind was in high gear, and I couldn't stop my consciousness from being flooded with thoughts and images of alien encounters. The three-hour drive passed in a blur. Later, I would wonder if had stopped at red lights and obeyed the highway laws.

I parked the car in the shade of a large maple tree and gazed at my house, the scene of so many disturbing encounters. I was exhausted. I knew so much more about aliens than when I left two days ago—and I must have replayed it all in my mind on the drive home. I wondered what my life would be like now. Would it be different?

I sat in the car for a while, staring at the house that symbolized all my feelings of insecurity and victimization. "The aliens are real!" I said aloud, trying to muster my courage. I was determined to survive, and reclaim my life. Finally, I took a deep breath, got out of the car and unlocked the front door. I reminded myself that "we fear what we don't understand." With Barbara's help, I was learning to understand the aliens; perhaps I would learn that my contacts with them weren't totally negative. Then the door closed behind me, and I reentered my life.

The following months were particularly difficult. Less than a week after I returned, my best friend died unexpectedly. The day before he died, he told me and his doctor that a large ball of light had hovered outside the window of his hospital room the previous night. "It was an alien craft," he said. "Did anyone else see it?" He also told me that aliens had visited his room several times. As he was waiting to be released from the hospital, his heart suddenly failed. My confidence crashed; I expected to be next.

Rather than building my strength, I turned inward and became very insular. The aliens had me to themselves. Barbara and I talked on the telephone once or twice a week, and I made frequent trips to see her. But physical and emotional fatigue was consuming the joy of my life.

Another friend died exactly six months after my first visit with Barbara. His mysterious death may also have been related to alien visitations. His wife confided in me that a large craft had landed in front of their house a few months earlier. She was sure that aliens had entered their home many times—and she had had abduction experiences similar to mine.

I couldn't understand why two of my best friends had been taken so abruptly. Both were healthy, happy young men. Their deaths plunged me deep into fear and depression. Night after sleepless night, I escaped thoughts of aliens by planning my own suicide. In retrospect, my solitude simply assured the aliens that I would be readily available for their visits.

During the second week of February 1993, I was admitted to the hospital, where I lay in a feverish, comatose state for nearly a week. No one expected me to live.

Barbara, Jane, and other friends visited me, and prayed for my survival. The doctors speculated that the fever had damaged my brain, but Jane's psychic intuitions didn't agree. "He'll live and be vital again," she assured Barbara. In fact, she predicted that afterward I would be physically larger and psychically stronger. As Jane and Barbara were leaving my room one morning, Jane touched Barbara's arm and said, "Jim's been taken down by the aliens for reprogramming. They're restructuring his body."

The physicians conducted several medical tests, including a spinal tap, but none of their tests produced a conclusive diagnosis of my illness. When the fever finally subsided, my family physician wrote "viremia" on my medical chart, and said to my mother, "Jim must've had some unusual influenza virus."

I didn't tell the doctors or my family about the alien beings who had entered my bedroom just before I got sick. They projected a beam of light into my body, just below the navel, and the feverish symptoms had manifested immediately afterward. I struggled to maintain consciousness until they left. Then I called a neighbor, saying, "Maggie, I'm very sick." After seeing me, she called the doctor, and her husband rushed me to the emergency room. My temperature was 106.

My long sleep ended as abruptly as it began. When I regained consciousness, one of the nurses was at my side. I was surprised to still be alive and in my body. I began to cry, telling her that I did not want to live. "Alien beings made me sick, and surrounded my bed while I was asleep," I sobbed.

She squeezed my hand supportively, and said, "I had a similar experience a few years ago. I'm glad I was with you when you returned. I believe you."

The happy sight of Barbara and Jane gave me strength. Barbara couldn't wait to tell me Jane's predictions. I responded, "You're right. Not only will I survive—I'm going to write a book." Although my mind was still clouded, I knew that I was going to write a book about my encounters with aliens.

A crippling snowstorm devastated the area, and the hospital had to switch to emergency generator power. As a result, some patients were discharged early, including me. My friends Janet and Peter offered to take me home in their four-wheel-drive vehicle. The city was hidden beneath deep snow; the streets and many of the houses had practically disappeared. As Peter cautiously guided his vehicle toward my house, I thought, *How fitting!* Most of my conscious memories had vanished in the fever—and now I couldn't even recognize my own hometown.

I stayed in my neighbors' guest bedroom for nearly a week. I was too weak to care for myself, and I couldn't face being alone in my cavernous old house. Like family and friends, my house seemed unfamiliar. I had to become reacquainted with my entire world.

Physically, my recovery only took two weeks, but my mental recovery took much longer. When I returned to work, everything in my office was unfamiliar. I quickly learned how to fake my way through conversations, and I had to re-read documents and files before I could answer a question or make a decision. Only Barbara knew about my memory loss. Everyone else probably thought that I was just acting strange because of my illness.

My memory didn't return for nearly nine months, and by the time it returned I had to go out and buy larger shoes and clothing. This part of Jane's prediction was definitely true. She was also right about my psychic abilities. My father died a few weeks after I was released from the hospital. When he died, he was hospitalized in Arkansas, and I was traveling in Texas. At the exact moment that he crossed into spirit life, I heard him say, "That was easy!" Just moments later the phone rang—it was my sister saying that he had just died. This verified my ability to communicate with the other side.

After my recovery, Barbara and I discussed book ideas for several months. She encouraged, and I procrastinated—I didn't want to relive my alien encounters. When Barbara met my friend Kyle in the summer of 1993, they formed an alliance, and he began the tedious process of transcribing the regression videos and telephone tapes. "Barbara and I will help, and the three of us can produce a book!" he assured me.

The aliens seemed anxious for me to write about my interdimensional experiences. For nearly a year after my first abduction, I was haunted by my memories of the telepathic voice and the trip to the subterranean facility. I sometimes felt like a radio tuned a distant station. Were the aliens preparing me to write about my experiences with them?

I began to see their intrusions into my life from a new perspective. I wondered about their motives for prodding me to accept their existence and seek to understand their link with humans. Kyle and Barbara continued to be helpful. During one of our conversations about the book, Kyle said, "Your story will be helpful to people who are struggling to understand their own alien abductions."

For the first year and a half, I was hesitant to discuss my alien encounters. As I studied Kyle's growing mound of tape transcripts, however, I began to think that the aliens might have selected—or even programmed—me to inform a larger audience of their existence. I spent many solitary hours wondering how to tell my story.

During the first hypnotic regression, Barbara had opened my subconscious, and gradually, more repressed information had worked its way into my awareness. Thoughts about my role as a communicator worked their way through my fear and confusion. Eventually, I dedicated myself to the dissolution of the veil between humans and aliens. After nearly three years of thinking about aliens, with the help of Kyle and Barbara, a book about my alien odyssey began to form in my mind.

In December 1994, I organized all my transcripts in a large binder. When it was done, I sat by the fireplace one cold winter evening and thumbed through it. I realized how overwhelming the material was. I couldn't just write that "Humans are sharing Earth with alien beings of superior intelligence and technology." I would have to write the story from beginning to end, but how to do it? I reminded myself that writing is the final step in the intellectual process—the last step, after collecting, processing, and analyzing information.

However, I soon found that this advice is based on human logic—which doesn't apply to aliens. When I tried to analyze my experiences, asking "Why or how did they do that?" I found it to be a waste of time. I couldn't comprehend their motives or methods. Human thought is so far removed from alien intelligence that we simply can't use logic to analyze our encounters with them. Before I could transform my ideas into words, I had to overhaul my way of thinking.

The traditional research model that I had learned in graduate school also turned out to be inadequate for the task. I could define the problem, collect descriptive information, analyze it, and develop interesting theories. But I couldn't produce any empirical data or evidence to support my claims. Seeking proof of the existence of alien beings, I put off writing the book for another year. I assumed that a book about aliens wouldn't have much credibility unless it could provide concrete evidence of their existence.

Apparently, aliens can transcend time, transform matter, and manipulate human thought and behavior. They can also create distracting illusions to satisfy the needs of our simple human minds. As far as I know, they have never left verifiable evidence of their visits to our dimension, or of human visits to their dimension. Eventually I realized the futility of waiting for verifiable evidence, and decided to write about my experiences anyway.

I had survived hundreds of alien contacts, and had thousands of memory fragments to piece together. My binder was bulging with transcripts and notes. Also, Barbara had carefully researched and documented my life, and was available to guide me into my subconscious. So the greatest challenge was deciding what to leave out. I finally started writing in January 1995.

Barbara encouraged me to have faith in myself, and assured me that my information would be valuable to other people. She encouraged me to accept that some people wouldn't believe or understand me. "Jim, your accounts of interdimensional journeys will become more relevant as others report similar experiences, and ask the same questions you've asked."

Beginning the book initiated a long process of organizing and clarifying my thoughts. I became increasingly convinced that aliens had prepared me—and others—to bring our respective worlds closer together. As I commented to Barbara in one of our sessions, "Our questions about aliens will eventually open our minds to other dimensions."

My ideas for the book evolved during the four years that I waited to write. First I had wanted to warn others about the atrocities of alien abductions. But as I overcame my victim consciousness, I started a more positive—albeit unsuccessful—quest to prove the existence of aliens. Ultimately, I realized that we must learn what we can from each alien encounter. Therefore, my purpose is simply to encourage human questioning about aliens, and their relationship with us.

My understanding of alien beings is still evolving. Each new encounter initiates more questions. The remaining chapters present my thoughts, theories, and experiences about the aliens, as I perceive them currently.

Part Two

7 | HUMAN HYBRIDS

WHEN MY alien abductors first said, "You are not who you think you are, and you must accept this," I didn't understand what it meant. I could only relate it to my human life. "Who else could I be?" I asked naively.

The idea that aliens might be producing human-alien hybrids never occurred to me until Barbara guided me into hypnosis, and I saw my embryo in a glass cylinder. As I observed the creation of my life by alien scientists, I understood that thousands of years of alien experimentation had culminated in extensive human hybridization programs, ranging from intellectual creativity to maniacal behaviors.

As I recognized my embryo in the glass cylinder, the proverbial light bulb flashed in my mind. I was told that an extraterrestrial race had colonized this planet during its pristine period. The interdimensional alien beings came to harvest Earth's natural resources, employ its primitive human population, and harness its energies. The intelligent beings who descended to Earth used early humans as laborers and energy sources. Just as human scientists have developed animals for nourishment, labor, and entertainment purposes, alien scientists have improved humans for the same reasons—and possibly others.

As I looked at the startling image of my embryo, a distant voice discussed my creation. "Your mother, and her mother, and her mother were created this way," the voice explained. "Human hybrids have been used successively to produce more advanced hybrid beings." I understood that alien scientists have used hybrids to gradually increase human intelligence.

"Did I receive special benefits because I was incubated in my mother's hybrid womb?"

"You are an improved variation of her strain."

After the voice spoke to me, I thought about my brothers and sisters. I wondered if two of my sisters and one of my brothers might also be human hybrids.

Occasionally, I will recognize an indefinable essence in another person, which causes me to wonder if they are also a hybrid. This inexplicable sense of recognition is beyond my feelings, psychic intuitions, or knowledge of their life; it is not a response to their physical appearance or personal characteristics.

It was a few days after the 1992 election, as I was riding a bus, that I first recognized a fellow human hybrid. Five athletic men were jogging toward the slow, ambling bus. One man was in the center, while the other four formed a protective square around him. The man in the center looked up and made riveting eye contact with me. I recognized his handsome face. He had just been elected to a high government position.

For an instant our eyes connected, and I glimpsed another world. Inwardly, I exclaimed, *I recognize you! You're one of them. You're a human hybrid*. The fleeting encounter was over in three or four seconds but it had been a profound learning experience. As I turned in my seat to watch the joggers pass, I had to ask myself, *Are the aliens programming human hybrids to assume control of the world?*

I've had several similar encounters with strangers, in which I have a deep inner sense of recognition of someone, and my mind transcends the boundaries of our world.

If I'm typical, most hybrids don't have any conscious knowledge of their interdimensional creation or alien programming, at least until they're hypnotized, as I was.

In addition to their general life orientation, each human hybrid also receives more specialized programming. The aliens explained my service orientation to me, and allowed me to view my creation from the biological and ethereal components of the three corpses. I realized that these donors had contributed specialized ingredients for my life. I don't know what the two men contributed, but I'm sure that the woman supplied enhanced psychic sensitivity.

I don't have a clear image of her, other than gray hair. But we are still mentally connected, and she has communicated with me telepathically. Her first message was: "We share the same mind, although my human body expired before your creation." I interpreted this to mean that I received my psychic abilities from her.

I used to think that everyone has latent psychic abilities that they can learn to develop. But now I think that only some hybrids are psychic. I also wonder if some psychics have alien programming devices implanted in their physical or interdimensional bodies.

I assume that alien scientists have improved their human engineering technologies over the past forty or fifty years, just as human technology has advanced. If so, their new hybrids may be far more advanced than my contemporaries and I. This idea makes me feel old—like an antique model of a hybrid.

Alien scientists seem able to determine all our characteristics—including our personality, intelligence, creativity, and physical features. In addition, they seem able to activate our programming at a specific time and to propel us into predetermined events. For example, what if alien scientists have developed a charismatic human hybrid and programmed this person to become the president of the United States in 2008?

Human hybrids are programmed to interface with other human hybrids at the time and place predetermined by alien scientists. In fact, when human-hybrid embryos are created and programmed, all their interactions and relationships may also be planned. Our romantic relationships and professional associations, for example, may be programmed in our embryos. Alien scientists strategically locate hybrids in communities around the globe—and some communities or nations may be occupied by more hybrids.

I believe that aliens must examine their hybrids periodically to evaluate their progress, and that human contacts with aliens are escalating, because aliens are entering our dimension more frequently to monitor us. They can also use our implant devices to adjust our life-orientation programming.

During one of my visits with Barbara, she asked me to watch the video of a delightful little girl, about eight or nine years old. A friend of the girl's family had asked Barbara to investigate a report of a mass alien abduction. The girl's conscious memories of the encounter were very clear—she calmly explained to Barbara how alien beings had taken her and many of her neighbors onto an alien spaceship.

According to the information that Barbara collected from the girl and her neighbors, a troop of alien beings invaded many homes in the neighborhood at night and took people of all ages to a central location, which they perceived as a spaceship. Barbara was particularly interested in the case because many members of the neighborhood had conscious memories of being taken onto the alien spacecraft. In addition, she was impressed by the girl's calm explanation of the details of the abduction. In a heavy Southern accent, she said, "I'd never seen alien beings until that night. I never thought about being on a spaceship until the aliens arrived at my house and took me to theirs."

From time to time, Barbara would stop the video and ask for my reaction to the girl's story. "Why would an entire neighborhood be invaded by alien beings, and why would groups of people be taken aboard a spaceship?" she wondered.

I responded, "After listening to the little girl's observations, I think the abductees were being reminded of their interdimensional origins. I didn't understand either my life or my contact with aliens until I discovered that I was a human hybrid and accepted my interdimensional connections."

"Do the aliens want certain people to know that they are human hybrids?"

"I think so. The spaceship may have been real, or it may have been an alien-manipulated illusion that the abductees' human minds could accept. In my opinion, the purpose of the mass abduction was to introduce the girl and her neighbors to their interdimensional origins."

"This was a daring operation by the abductors."

"Yes, and we should expect more mass abductions. The aliens are encouraging us to start accepting ourselves as hybrid humans." Feeling confident about my theory, I added, "The abductees were probably examined and given checkups—and programming implants may have been installed, as well. The roundup was an orientation, examination, and socialization process—an opportunity for the human hybrids to meet their own kind."

"Your theory is very interesting."

"In a way, a mass abduction is like a reunion, in which human hybrids are reunited with their alien creators."

"Are all the abductees hybrids?"

"All of them!" I said confidently. "Although they live in the same neighborhood, they probably don't know each other as humans—but they must share a common interdimensional heritage."

"If so, how will their lives be affected by the mass abduction?"

"After meeting in the alien dimension, they'll begin to recognize something familiar in each other as they interact in the human world, which may create bonds among them."

For example, I assume that fellow abductees will eventually play important roles in the little girl's future. They might be her future teachers, business partners, or lovers. I reiterated, "Those who shared the mass abduction were brought together to gain understanding of themselves and their own kind."

I also had a new theory: "These people may be the subjects of a single specialized experiment. The aliens may have strategically positioned them in one neighborhood so they could more easily collect them and guide their common purpose. They might share some programming that would cause them to think alike or flock together for some purpose."

The little girl's account of her abduction was also of interest to me because it closely paralleled my own experiences.

She spoke emphatically of being on "an uncomfortable bench" and described the "suction-cup fingers" on the aliens' hands—both of which I had experienced. She then raised her hand to the side of her head, grimaced and said, "Something busted in my head." To me, this was a sure sign that a programming device had been implanted in her head. Unlike me, however, she didn't appear to be emotionally traumatized by the experience.

Barbara remarked, "This child has almost complete conscious recall of her experience in the other dimension. When I interviewed her, I felt I was recording very valuable information about alien activities."

"Yes," I agreed. "I listened carefully to her account, and it seemed to validate almost everything I said in my first regression."

As I listened to the calm, sincere little girl, another question came to mind. Could she be an example of a new, improved human hybrid?

After all, I was forty-five before I had my first conscious alien-abduction memories—and was deeply traumatized by them. The little girl was eight or nine, and seemed quite cheerful and accepting. She spoke freely of being taken from her home, and wasn't disturbed about being on the spaceship. To support her account, she calmly drew pictures of the aliens and their ship.

I felt old. "My awakening was so much more difficult than hers. I'm barely forty years older, and she's so much further advanced."

"Yes," Barbara said. "She may be a new model."

"The hybrids of my generation have been emotionally crippled by their alien contacts, but younger people don't seem to experience that kind of emotional trauma. If this little girl represents a new generation, we can conclude that the new models don't fear alien beings. Their interdimensional connections may be more refined than ours, or more natural to them. Moreover, the new hybrids seem to know themselves better. This girl has both a positive attitude toward alien beings and a healthy sense of self-acceptance."

"You may be right. The younger human hybrids may be more capable of bridging the gap between the dimensions."

Although our alien encounters were similar, the girl was able to consciously report her abduction; I had to be hypnotized to retrieve the details. When she described her abductors, she showed no stress; I cried for months. She defended the aliens, saying, "They would be mean for only one reason. People have never been nice to them."

I asked Barbara, "In the beginning, did I ever defend aliens?"

Barbara shook her head and pursed her lips. We were both thinking that the little girl understood our alien creators much better than I had.

So, who are the hybrids, and why have alien scientists devoted thousands of years to developing them? I would love to provide factual answers to these questions. However, our only sources of information are the fragments that have surfaced in the minds of people like me and the little girl. Nevertheless, a few individuals—like Barbara—have dedicated their lives to documenting and piecing together the fragments of the alien-abduction puzzle—"the big game board," as she calls it.

It's logical to want to explain human hybrids and determine who they might be, but it's difficult to discuss a theory that most people have never considered. Most of my ideas about hybrids came from my own hypnotic regressions, so I wanted to use information from other sources. At first I couldn't think of any, but then I realized that I had another key resource—Barbara. When I asked her if we could get together to exchange ideas, she agreed enthusiastically. Kyle decided to participate, too, and we met at her house on a Saturday afternoon. It was like so many of our other meetings, except that this time, I would be guiding the interview.

I started the conversation by saying, "In my first and second regressions, we recorded a great deal of information about my creation, and we've discussed your interview with the little girl. But I'd like to supplement this with other sources. How did *you* acquire your ideas about human hybrids?"

She replied, "My information began with my understanding of myself…the basic understanding of how I'm different from the human crowd."

"Have you discovered anything about human hybrids that sets them apart from other human beings?"

Barbara responded, "Based on the hundreds of abduction cases I've documented and analyzed, I do recognize some qualities and patterns of life experience that set abductees apart from other people. But, according to my theory, everyone on Earth is a potential contactee."

I'd never considered that possibility before. "If that's correct, we shouldn't assume that everyone who is contacted or abducted by alien beings is a hybrid."

"And," Kyle said, "those who are fascinated by alien beings and UFOs may not necessarily be hybrids, either. After all, Jim didn't have any interest in aliens until he was abducted—yet now he believes he's a hybrid."

"Maybe we could identify human hybrids with the 'batch-consignment theory,'" Barbara said. "You came up with this idea in your first regression, when you suggested that some hybrids may come into life in batches."

Kyle looked puzzled, and Barbara explained, "In his first regression, Jim mentioned the increasing number of children with a propensity for evil, lack of conscience, and violence. I interpreted this to mean that aliens have developed batches of genetically altered children, programmed with certain criminal behavior. Right now, gangs are proliferating—are these children being 'batched' into life by aliens?"

She continued, "Jim, on the other hand, is from the 'intuitive' batch."

"That means," Kyle reasoned, "that anyone could be a hybrid, and we don't have enough information to second-guess the aliens' motives for creating such a wide spectrum of human behavior."

"Yes," Barbara said. "The question is, 'Who's here to do what?'"

I agreed—we can't yet identify human hybrids with certainty. "Human hybrids must discover themselves and learn to recognize one another."

I believe that human hybrids are experimentally programmed by alien scientists to exhibit specific behaviors, or facilitate predetermined events. In other words, alien scientists are experimenting with every possible aspect of human intelligence, behavior, and emotion. Therefore, anyone from a national leader to a violent gang member could be a hybrid.

Then Barbara described her "Hatfield & McCoy Polarity Game" theory: "According to this theory, the aliens program human hybrids into polarized groups and manipulate them into opposing one another. For example, I've hypnotized many abductees who've had disturbing dreams about Nazis. Some dreamt about being a Nazi; others dreamt of being victimized by Nazis. But all of them could recall specific information about past lives in Nazi Germany."

I wondered, "Were the Nazi leaders a human hybrid control group, with alien-programmed objectives? Were they an alien-directed experimental group developed to oppose other human groups? If so, for what purpose?"

"We can't outguess the aliens' motives," Kyle reminded me. "But if your theories are correct, alien scientists may be orchestrating many world events through their manipulations of human hybrids."

I agreed. "Yes. This may be one reason why we're not allowed to readily identify human hybrids. We'll be asking, 'Who are the hybrids?' until the aliens are ready for us to know, and to understand how they're changing our world."

8 | WHO ARE THE HULIENS?

HUMAN HYBRIDS on Earth are part human and part alien—but I believe that alien scientists are also creating another group of hybrids, which I call "interdimensional hybrids," or "interdimensionals." Like human hybrids, the interdimensionals have both human and alien qualities; the difference is that they live in other dimensions. When I was preparing to write about hybrids, Kyle offered to brainstorm ideas with me. My tongue slipped as we were talking, and I called them "huliens." The new word lingered in my thoughts, and I finally decided that huliens is a distinctive designation for the human-alien hybrids who reside in the alien dimension.

It's true that the technology and scope of interdimensional alien research is beyond our comprehension. However, this book would be incomplete if I didn't at least offer what I know about this subject.

My awareness of interdimensionals is based on my perceptions of those I've met—they seem to share their creators' ability to transcend dimensions. My first visit with an interdimensional hybrid occurred over a year after I was mated interdimensionally. I was home alone on a Saturday afternoon, resting in bed on a handmade quilt. Suddenly all my senses were heightened—I became acutely aware of the colors, fibers, and stitching in the quilt. I didn't understand what was happening, but everything around me seemed intensified and magnified. I curled up in a fetal position, with my head at the foot of the bed, when the interdimensional woman entered my bedroom.

I don't recall seeing her pass through a door or wall, like the alien with the red eye. She just materialized in the middle of the room, near the foot of the bed. Her face was humanlike, but her features were rather distorted, and her skin was pale and transparent. She had thick, coarse blonde hair that fell straight to her shoulders, like a mop. She wore a seamless, diaphanous silvery garment with long sleeves that draped at her wrists. She extended her arms, as if reaching out to me. Then I saw that she was holding a little boy—and as I watched, she gently laid him on the bed beside me. Then she stepped back and assumed a vigilant position in the middle of the room.

He was also blonde and pale, and looked about six months old. He crawled onto me immediately, as if he knew me and had played with me before. I felt like a proud parent. He looked like a normal six-month-old child—except for one unusual feature. His teeth were fully developed, and he also had narrow teeth in the back of his mouth, extending down from the roof of his mouth. (I've thought about this many times, but still can't offer a plausible explanation for it.)

While the little boy and I played happily, the woman watched, as if standing guard. Time seemed to stand still. I remember asking the woman, "Where do you live?" She did not answer or move a muscle. She was stone-faced, expressionless, as if she was a robot incapable of communication. Her only emotional gesture was her tender delivery of the child to me. For several days afterward, I had the lingering feeling that she had telepathically placed thoughts in my mind, but I couldn't retrieve them.

When she arrived, and while I played with the child, I was fully conscious. But within thirty minutes or so I became very drowsy, and I lost consciousness before they left, so I don't remember their departure. Perhaps the woman used her superior mental power to induce anesthesia in me. When I awoke, I felt an overwhelming sense of loneliness. I wanted to be with my son; I wasn't ready for him to leave me. And I needed to know more about him.

Feeling as if I'd lost a child, I was despondent for several days. I longed for some kind of contact or communication with the child's human mother. Instead, I called Barbara. As usual, she was there when I needed her—and as I described my visitors, I could hear the excitement in her voice. "You're reporting very important new information," she said.

In response to her questions, I pressed my mind for every possible intuition. *The woman is the child's surrogate mother; like other interdimensional children, he lives in a protected interdimensional environment.* I wondered how I had acquired these thoughts. *Did the interdimensional woman explain this to me?*

However, I couldn't answer all of Barbara's questions. At one point, I was so frustrated that I shouted, "They were real! They entered my conscious reality! They were in my bedroom!"

Because of my intense paternal feelings, I felt sure that the child was the product of my interdimensional union, and I struggled to understand how such a beautiful child could have resulted from such a disturbing experience. First I had assumed that we had produced an embryo, which was then removed from her body. Then I saw scenes of the child developing in a glass cylinder. Then I wondered whether the woman's interdimensional body could have given birth to him. I even wondered if his embryo had been implanted into the interdimensional woman. However, I couldn't come up with a good explanation for the boy's existence. My only relief was to share his visit with Barbara.

For days, thoughts of him filled my mind. I asked many questions, but received no convincing answers. I loved him, and wanted to be with him. I tried to imagine the interdimensional nursery and wondered how many other interdimensional children had been created. I kept asking, "Why was this child created?" and was terribly disturbed by the thought that I might never see him again.

Several months passed, and my pain began to fade. I could never erase the memory of holding him, but I gradually lost hope of ever seeing him again. Then, without any warning, I was taken to him.

The journey began at night. I was asleep when two alien beings removed me from my bed, without disturbing my sleep. I next remember standing in front of a wide doorway, like an elevator entrance; the large, dark door was closed. I stared at the door, as if entranced. Then I came to life, and asked, "What's on the other side of these doors?"

I looked to my left and right. I wasn't alone; two gray aliens were escorting me, one on either side. Their eyes weren't glowing, but otherwise they were like the aliens I'd met before, only a bit shorter; their heads didn't quite reach my shoulders.

The door opened in the middle, and they gestured for me to step forward. I stepped through the doorway and onto a shiny semi-circular platform, large enough for all of us. As my feet came to rest on it, another platform moved into place just below. I followed their instructions to step down again, and yet another platform emerged—and so it went. I realized that we were descending into a subterranean facility.

The last step took me into a lavishly decorated Victorian-style parlor. As soon as my eyes adjusted to the bright lighting, I noticed beautiful red walls. Then I saw an old man, dressed in clothing that humans might have worn a hundred years ago. As he extended his hand and ushered me into the parlor, the two gray beings vanished.

As he welcomed me, I was attracted to a large, brilliant "ring" on one of his fingers. *What a magnificent ruby,* I thought. But as I gazed into its mesmerizing glow, a familiar thought arose from deep in my mind: *Oh! I recognize you. You're one of them.*

The old man had the same facial features as the interdimensional woman who had visited me. His face appeared human, but it was scarred and contorted. He seemed more solid, less transparent, than the woman. His welcoming gestures were pleasant; I felt at ease with him immediately. He didn't speak, but his movements directed my attention to my left.

The interdimensional woman was sitting on a Victorian settee, and I recognized her at once. Although her face was frozen and unsmiling, I sensed that she was glad to see me. She looked downward, and my eyes followed her gaze. The little boy was standing on wobbly legs. His back was to me, and he was holding onto her leg for support.

He turned around, and our eyes met. He seemed to recognize me in the same heartfelt way that I recognized him. He was learning to walk, and took an unsteady step toward me, recovering his balance as our hands met. *My child!* I thought.

I lifted him to my chest and embraced him. His pale, nearly white skin felt soft and smooth, but was much cooler than mine. As we played with one another, the woman sat quietly and watched us. I sensed that this time she trusted me—she knew that I wouldn't harm him.

I don't know how long I was there. My memory of our time in the parlor fades into a feeling of holding him quietly. As before, I must have been anesthetized when it was time to leave, and I had no memory of being returned to bed. But when I awoke, the ornate Victorian parlor was still vivid in my mind's eye. The interdimensional man and woman had seemed out of place in it. I wondered if the aliens had created the Victorian setting to comfort me, or so that the boy and I could play together in a human environment.

I tossed and turned the rest of the night. My parental longing overpowered my need for sleep—I wanted to be with my child. Why did the aliens let me experience the playful affection of a little boy who lives in a world apart from me? Why did they encourage me to feel like a loving parent? These questions, and others, kept racing through my mind.

These interdimensional visits stumped me; I didn't have any theories to account for them. At first I thought the aliens wanted the boy to experience human affection, possibly to absorb human qualities—but there were other possibilities, as well. I asked Barbara, "Could he be a prototype for interdimensionals who can feel human emotions? Or were the alien scientists simply studying my emotional reactions and parental instincts?"

I'm still filled with questions about my interdimensional son's future. I wonder where he'll live when he grows up, and what he'll be or do. Usually, I have no answers, but sometimes I get an insight. Once I thought, *He may be living somewhere on Earth. He may have been placed in a human body, as a walk-in. Our visits may have been socialization experiences, to help him adjust. Maybe we've enjoyed other times together, which I can't remember.* Another time, I wondered if alien scientists produced a duplicate of each hybrid life. One counterpart might live in our dimension, while the other one lives in theirs—and the duplicates could be interchangeable. These ideas may have been wishful thinking on my part, fueling the hope that I would meet my son someday. But I could see how an interdimensional could be installed in a human body when a human hybrid's essence was taken to the alien dimension for adjustment.

Such questions about my interdimensional son actually helped me to discover the distinction between human hybrids and interdimensionals. Also, while thinking of him one evening, I suddenly began to have frightful thoughts about the humans I had seen in the underground laboratory—and another piece of the puzzle fell into place.

Except for his teeth, my son looked very human. During my first regression, I thought that the humans I had seen in the laboratory were volunteers, working cooperatively with aliens. Under the bright overhead lights, they looked human; and at the time, I didn't know about hybrids yet. But now I wondered whether they were human hybrids or interdimensionals—and this question opened up vast new possibilities.

Many people believe that our government has made agreements with aliens and allowed them to develop an extensive network of subterranean bases. I started to think about those who could have executed such agreements. Could some of our top government officials be human hybrids or interdimensional walk-ins? Could they have been programmed by aliens to fulfill their master plan for humanity? And could some hybrids live in both dimensions?

When I met the old man with the glowing red "ruby" on his finger, I recalled the humans in the underground facility who had glowing red control devices under their fingernails. Now I wondered if all these devices could be the same technology as the glowing red eye of my first alien abductor. I concluded that at least some of the humans in the underground facility must have been human hybrids or interdimensionals.

I can only offer my theories about interdimensionals, because they have left verifiable evidence of their existence. However, my friend Tina believes that my "hulien" son is real—because she saw him!

On February 9, 1997, at least three years after my trip to the Victorian park, he appeared in my living room. I was doing stretching exercises on the floor when I looked up and saw him watching me. At first I was startled and didn't recognize him. He had grown! His body was stocky and the size of a five- or six-year-old child. His head was larger than a human head, and his face looked like a teenager's. His blonde hair was thick and coarse, like a mop, and his eyebrows were bushy. He was dressed in red. He didn't speak, but I sensed his need for me to recognize him. Just as I was about to speak, the telephone rang, and he vanished.

Two days later, Tina called and asked if she could stop by for a visit with a friend from out of town. While they were getting settled in the living room, I offered to make a pot of tea. Tina is wellknown for her ability to "see" psychically and has provided psychic counseling for many people.

When I returned to the living room, Tina was entranced. I was surprised, because she'd never gone into a trance before. Then she spoke, describing my son and saying that he was in the room. She pointed to three areas of the room where he had appeared to her. She called him the "Dear One." "He's concerned," she said. "He thinks you don't like his hair."

I was stunned. When he appeared two days before, I had in fact had critical thoughts about his unruly hair—but there was no way Tina could have known that. Her unexpected message was a confirmation of my interdimensional son's existence. I think of him often, and hope that he will come for other visits. I'd like him to teach me more about interdimensionals.

9 | LOVE OBSESSIONS

WHEN I discuss my theories about hybrid beings, most people can't resist asking, "Am I a human hybrid?" I'm hesitant to answer such questions, because my perceptions might be wrong. Instead, I encourage people to ask their own questions and form their own opinions about aliens and hybrid humans.

Some hybrids may never become aware of their alien origin; but I believe that an increasing number of people will soon be hearing alien wake-up calls, and asked to accept their alien heritage. I've developed the following list of questions based on my own experiences. Perhaps other hybrids who are programmed to discover their alien connections will find that they will answer "yes" to most of them:

When you were a child, did you feel presences or
see beings?

Were you sexually molested as a child?

Have you dreamt of being in underground facilities?

Have you dreamt of medical examinations?

Have you dreamt of being taken onto spaceships?

Have you ever experienced significant memory losses or lost-time episodes?

Have you ever felt as if information has been forced into your brain?

Have you seen or encountered UFOs?

Have you every had psychic or paranormal experiences?

Have you ever been involved in unrequited, obsessive love relationships?

It may come as a surprise, but I've found that traumatic love obsessions may be one of the strongest clues that a person is a human hybrid. I also believe that many people who are trapped in unfulfilled love obsessions are actually starring in alien-directed dramas.

Love obsessions have played a major role in my life, and I believe that a book about aliens would be incomplete without some consideration of them. But initially I doubted my ability to explain the relationship between human love obsessions and alien manipulation of humans. So one hot summer day, I met with Kyle and Barbara to share our ideas about love obsessions. We seated ourselves on Barbara's patio, in the shade of a large cottonwood tree, overlooking the ducks in her backyard pond. All the drakes were in pursuit of one elegantly feathered, demure water ballerina. Our humorous comments about the drakes' antics set the stage for our discussion about alien-manipulated love obsessions.

Telling other people about one's most intimate love obsessions feels like stripping one's clothes off in front of them. But the ducks inspired us, and soon we were speaking candidly about our love obsessions, and wondering why so many people were preoccupied with unrequited love affairs.

Barbara volunteered to share some of her ideas about love obsessions. "The alien intelligence," she began, "knows how every part of our body works. It is intimately attuned to all our mental and physical functions. The aliens can program all our emotional responses to produce misery, jealousy, passion, or love. I know from my personal experience, as well as my research, that alien scientists program many people for love obsessions—and can even program us to search for specific companions or mates."

Kyle and I agreed. "I've suffered from several long, painful love obsessions," I confessed. "Some were emotional whirlwinds, and they lasted for years. In college, I was obsessed with a graduate student who arrived in the cafeteria at the same time every morning. I fell in love at first sight, and those obsessive emotions consumed my life. I was miserable for two years. My heart ached, because my love wasn't returned, or even noticed!"

"You watched this person eat breakfast every morning for two years?" Kyle asked. "What were you thinking?"

"Mostly sexual fantasies," I admitted. "And they surpassed any physical possibilities!"

Love obsessions can be crippling. They can sap our strength and destroy our life. They can wreck our relationships and cause us to do irrational things. I was forty-five before I understood my obsessive life-long search for a Nordic lover who first appeared in my fantasies during adolescence. I believe now that alien scientists programmed that image in my mind when I was a child, but we didn't meet until I'd endured nearly thirty-five years of debilitating love obsessions and sexual fantasies. I had always fallen hopelessly in love with tall blondes—but my love had never been returned.

When I finally did meet my fantasy lover (whom I'll refer to as Lee) in real life, my world stood still. A friend and I sat down for dinner in a restaurant where Lee was working. He walked toward me and said, "What can I get for you?" and all I could think was "a lifetime together!"

This was four years before my first conscious alien abduction. I knew nothing yet about aliens, hybrids, or interdimensional lives. As far as I knew, my friend and I were just there to have a nice dinner. But it didn't work out like that. Lee's presence triggered thrilling—but confusing—thoughts in my mind, causing my heart to race. My fantasies were suddenly real. My friend tapped me on the shoulder and said, "You're staring!"

I *was* preoccupied. My head was filled with confusion at my powerful emotional reaction to this stranger. I knew we were well acquainted and that we had loved each other for a long time. Yet, we wouldn't meet again for nearly a year. We were both alone, and—although I didn't tell anyone how I felt—some mutual friends offered to introduce us. One friend told me, "You two have so much in common."

I declined their offers, thinking that we would get together eventually.

On a brisk October day, a year after our first encounter, Lee accepted an invitation to join me for lunch at a quaint little restaurant. I felt very nervous about having my first conversation with the person I'd loved for most of my life. I knew that my previous love obsessions had just been warm-ups compared to this one!

That day, we talked openly, and our friendship blossomed. We were close and caring at times, but avoided any sexual intimacy or talk of a relationship. Then Lee left town and was gone for nearly a year. We kept in touch with letters and phone calls while he was away. After returning, he stopped by for occasional visits, and our friendship continued like this for another year. During this time, my obsessive feelings diminished the quality of my life; I couldn't reconcile the vast differences between friendship and love obsession. I was depressed, preoccupied with sexual fantasies, and disturbed by the possibility of never fulfilling them.

Then, during my second hypnotic regression, nearly five years after I had first met Lee, Barbara suddenly asked me, "Why do you love Lee?"

My first response was, "I've never loved anyone as deeply," but I really didn't understand this myself. I was trying to say, "My feelings are different in some way. I feel obsessive and have a deep inner knowledge of Lee."

Barbara gave me a hypnotic suggestion to visualize walking down twenty steps, while thinking about Lee with each step. As I descended, I felt great emotional pressure growing within me. Suddenly, I exclaimed, "Part of me was taken to create Lee! I was very young, nine or ten—Lee was created from my flesh."

"Are you speaking literally?"

"Yes," I said, and began to cry.

Barbara asked me to explain, but I couldn't. I was numb. In response to her questions, I tried to talk, but the thoughts rushed through my mind faster than I could form words. I stammered, "It was done through tissue sampling...a piece of my flesh was removed...I have a scar." The aliens had taken a sample of my flesh to use in creating Lee.

I sat up, removed my sock, and looked at the scar on my left leg just above the ankle. "They took a tissue sample from my leg!" I said.

I had first noticed the open wound on a hot summer evening when I was nine or ten. It was a deep crater about the size of a nickel, through which my leg bone was visible. It didn't bleed or hurt; the flesh had simply vanished. My mother took me to a doctor, but I could never explain how the flesh had disappeared. This experience had always troubled me. I'd always felt that something significant happened, but I had no memory of it. "Lee was created from that tissue sample," I said slowly, trying to convince myself.

Barbara asked me to explain further. "Who removed the flesh from your leg?"

Still in shock, I couldn't answer. I was focused on my first glimpse of Lee in the restaurant. I was thinking of my initial feelings of recognition and my inability to explain my immediate, overwhelming love.

Barbara repeated her question more firmly. I responded, "Alien beings took the flesh from my leg and created the love connection between us. My love didn't come from my human side. Aliens programmed my feelings. Now, I understand why I didn't know how to express my love at first. Is this possible?"

"In my opinion," Barbara said, "aliens are perfectly capable of removing flesh from your body and using the tissue to create another person." Then, she asked, "What's the age difference between you?"

"Nine or ten years."

"The timing would be correct, then." She continued to question me about my obsession for Lee and my sexual fantasies.

"My fantasies of making love with Lee were more satisfying than any other sexual experiences I have had, or can imagine," I confessed.

However, I continued to have difficulty accepting this idea. I didn't want to believe that alien scientists had used my cells to develop Lee's embryo. I didn't recall seeing aliens when I was nine or ten, and I didn't know exactly when the flesh was removed from my leg. However, I did tell Barbara about a haunting lost-time episode.

On the day the crater appeared on my leg, I had been walking beside the house. "The east side of the house was shaded in the afternoon. I was there for a long time that day, but I can't remember why."

"Look again."

"The shady air was cooler around that corner of the house, and the grass was greener." I remembered the sensation of stepping onto the cool, damp grass. "Maybe I stepped through an alien doorway and walked into their dimension."

"Could the aliens have programmed the image of Lee in my mind when they removed the flesh?" I wondered. We both knew the answer. Alien intelligence is capable of accomplishing anything that our minds can conceive.

Barbara asked if I could remember any other details of this encounter, which might relate to my love obsession. "Oh, yes! Right after the crater appeared, I entered puberty and discovered masturbation. Also, the Nordic fantasy first appeared when I discovered the pleasure of my penis. I became increasingly obsessive about it. It was my primary masturbation fantasy...but could the aliens really have programmed us to meet thirty-five years later?"

"They may be quite capable of that."

After receiving this information, I was more certain than ever that Lee and I were involved in a love relationship. I didn't tell him about my regression, however. Barbara didn't want me to influence his thinking about alien contacts; I didn't want to appear crazy. But I did invite Lee to come with me when I went to see Barbara a few months later. By this time, he had mentioned his own alien encounters and Barbara was anxious to explore them.

Lee accepted Barbara's suggestions easily, and was soon in a trance—talking and acting like a three-year-old child. He spoke of getting out of bed at night, going to an open window, and looking into a bright light outside. When he entered it, that light turned out to be a beautiful playground in bright sunshine, where other kids and big people were playing.

Suddenly, Lee giggled, and said, "Jim is my friend!"

"You knew him at the playground?"

"He's a nice guy. I knew him when I was really young...a long time ago...before now."

"Tell me about Jim," Barbara pressed.

With uninhibited innocence and joy, Lee explained, "We were best friends; we held hands and laughed. We were naked a lot; it was funny."

Barbara asked where this was.

Lee replied, "In the same place"—the playground in the light.

"You met Jim in the sunny, green playground?"

"Yes! It had swings, and we used to swing. We ran, skipped, and held hands. We had so much fun! There was no one else who cared."

Barbara persisted, "Where was this place?"

"It's a beautiful playground. You know where it is. It's the secret place where special things happen. Big people and boys and girls play there."

"Is Jim your best friend?"

"Of course he is! He's my best friend! He's just my best friend! Then, abruptly, Lee's face looked very sad.

"What happened?"

"Jim went away one day, and I was really sad. I was afraid I would never see him again. I got mad and started to cry."

Barbara allowed Lee to cry for several minutes. Then he continued, "I miss Jim. He seems older now and doesn't have his dog anymore. He looks different—bigger than me."

Barbara suggested, "Jim's older now. Where do you see him?"

"I can only see his head, but he's smiling. He must be okay, but he can't talk to me. It must be all right for me to talk to him."

I was there during the regression, but I didn't speak, because my voice could interfere with Barbara's direction of Lee. I was glad to be there; Lee's childish voice and gestures were quite convincing. I could also remember haunting dreams of such a playground, which crept into my consciousness when I was twenty or twenty-one. I was a teenager by the time Lee was four or five and I would've seemed older to him. His mention of my dog was interesting. Because of school and part-time work, I gave Duke to a loving family when I was fourteen or fifteen. *We grew up thirteen hundred miles apart. How did he know about my dog?* I thought to myself. The session convinced me further that Lee and I knew each other from another time and dimension—that we loved each other long before we met in the restaurant.

Barbara asked Lee, "When did you see Jim again after he left the playground?"

"A long time. I didn't expect to see him again. I missed him. Did he miss me?"

The child Lee was innocent, unaware of what I'd said in my second regression. As Barbara brought Lee out of hypnosis, I scribbled down the following notes: "Did aliens implant Lee's image in my mind when they removed the tissue sample from my leg? As children, were we periodically taken to an interdimensional playground to become acquainted? Is this why I recognized Lee? Were we socialized with other hybrids? Did we share later abductions, which I haven't recalled? Were we programmed to meet thirty-five years later?" (Lee had moved to town, without knowing why, just before our meeting in the restaurant.) And, would the knowledge of our interdimensional relationship heal my love obsession?

After I recounted my obsession with Lee, Barbara, Kyle, and I continued to discuss love obsessions. After so many years of alien-abduction research, Barbara knows that an abductee's profile will also include love obsessions—and follow-up interviews with the abductees she has regressed reveal a surprising pattern. Most of them report significant changes in their relationships soon after they become aware of their interdimensional connections.

Some of them divorce and abruptly remarry; others are widowed and quickly find new partners. Those who are single before their abduction usually find partners soon afterward. These patterns suggest that abductions may include more than just checkups. Love-relationship programming may be altered or activated, and abductees may be programmed to find the mates created or selected by alien scientists. In fact, alien scientists appear to be fascinated with the emotional aspects of our consciousness.

Kyle asked, "Are aliens emotionless beings who find our emotions a curiosity? Are they attempting to instill emotions in their hybrids? Or, do they perhaps harvest energy or nourishment from our emotions?"

Love obsessions create highly charged emotions; there may be a link between the aliens' fascination with human emotions and human love obsessions. "Let's think about humans," I said, "as resources for aliens. What if our emotions provide fuel or nourishment for them?"

"Consider this," I continued. "Engineers routinely regulate the generation of electricity at hydroelectric plants by controlling the flow of water through turbines. Likewise, aliens could control the production of human emotions, or energies, by manipulating variables like love obsessions. If our emotions nourish or energize them in some way, they could turn us 'on' by activating our fantasies about unobtainable lovers."

"Your idea is interesting, but how do you explain the people who *do not* find fulfilling love relationships?" Barbara asked.

"Some hybrids may be created just for this purpose. They could work for the aliens most of their lives, without finding a fulfilling love relationship."

"That's interesting—how does your role as a sperm donor relate to this?"

"Human hybrid breeders may be prime candidates for alien-manipulated love obsessions. A person who's entangled in a love obsession is less likely to be sexually involved with a human partner."

"Good point," Barbara said.

"My obsessive feelings for Lee were most intense while I was being used as an interdimensional sperm donor. The aliens may have manipulated my obsession to facilitate their experiment. It would have assured them that I wouldn't be sexually involved in the human dimension, and would have kept me in an emotionally charged state of readiness."

During my first abduction, the aliens had extracted a semen sample, and other samples may have been taken as well. Barbara's research seems to indicate that semen extractions are a routine part of alien examination procedures. What do they do with all the samples? They may have purposes other than the creation of hybrid embryos. Or perhaps they analyze the samples to prepare for an interdimensional mating.

I suspect that human sperm is used to impregnate both human hybrid and interdimensional women. Barbara's research indicates that human women may serve as either short-term incubators or full-term hosts for hybrid embryos, and aliens may use love obsessions to control both male and female participants in their hybridization programs.

After a moment's silence, I said, "Making love in a human body is not as satisfying as making love in an inter-dimensional body."

Barbara and Kyle looked surprised. Barbara asked me to explain myself.

"Let's create a hypothetical situation," I said. "Barbara, you've developed a sexual fantasy about a handsome, virile man. He knows all your sexual desires and fulfills them masterfully. You don't know that aliens planted his image in your mind and charged your emotions. Your fantasy lover becomes very real to you, and expands the boundaries of your sexual gratification. You're consumed by a desire to be with him."

"Is he really tall, dark, and handsome?"

"He's perfect! He's the man of your dreams, literally. In the next phase, the aliens invade your home while you're sleeping, and take you—or your interdimensional body—to meet this manifestation of sexual perfection. They plan to develop a human-alien embryo in your body."

"Ouch! I see where this is headed."

"Yes. Your most thrilling sexual fantasies are fulfilled by your interdimensional lover. Now you're pregnant, but your conscious mind and body never know that. All you know is that you want to be with your fantasy lover."

"What happens next?" Kyle asked.

"Now, Barbara, your husband wants to make love to you—but you're no longer interested in him. You long for the perfect sexual gratification that you experienced in your interdimensional interlude, and reject your husband's advances. You may have retained some fleeting memories of your other lover, but you can't really explain your lack of interest in your husband. One thing leads to another, and before you know it, you're divorced. You have no conscious memory of being pregnant, and the aliens remove the embryo from your womb while you're sleeping."

"That scenario says a lot."

"Does this really happen?" Kyle asked.

"Yes, I think so. How could a person be satisfied with a human partner after their sexual fantasies have been fulfilled by an interdimensional lover? Human bodies are cumbersome compared to sex in the interdimensional body.

"I wonder if our sexual fantasies are being facilitated by interdimensional beings. Do they feel our sexual pleasure? Can they absorb sexual energy from us? Could this be another reason that aliens manipulate our love obsessions?

"People need to understand that we may not be creating and perpetuating these obsessions ourselves. If aliens are manipulating our emotions, we can't assume total responsibility, or guilt, for them. This may be the key to unlocking our love bondage."

"Knowledge is power," Barbara said. "Perhaps this will help others free themselves from unfulfilled love, or at least diminish their pain."

"When I think about love obsessions," I added, "I see an alien operating an old-fashioned telephone switchboard. The operator is connecting and disconnecting cords, the way the operator used to switch calls. But these cords connect people to people—each connection creates a love obsession, and each disconnection destroys a relationship. The alien operator is in control, manipulating human lives at will."

Although this analogy enabled us to end the session on a light note, we were still in the dark about why aliens would want to manipulate human emotions. However, we all believed that people would be less susceptible to this manipulation if they understood more about the subject.

10 | LET'S START OVER

FROM EARLY childhood, I always had a strong aversion to all forms of science fiction, and I never questioned these feelings. For more than forty years, I never read anything about UFOs or aliens, and I even avoided popular movies about extraterrestrials. The only exception was when a friend talked me into seeing *Close Encounters of the Third Kind*—but it had no impact on me; I just thought of it as a silly movie.

During the 1970s, like so many other young people, I explored Eastern metaphysics, and supplanted my Christian religious beliefs with ideas such as reincarnation, psychic phenomena, and spirits. At the same time, my psychic abilities emerged, and I acknowledged them as the gift of a benevolent God. For more than twenty years, I was comfortable with this understanding of life. But neither my Christian upbringing nor my metaphysical training prepared me for my first encounter with an interdimensional being.

During that first encounter, my first reaction was that the being must be an extraterrestrial from outer space. I figured that its spaceship was parked behind my house, and hoped my neighbors, Peter and Maggie, would see it—so that when the being carried me off to another planet, they would be able to report what had happened to me.

My understanding of aliens evolved slowly. At first, I assumed that I was the only person who had ever been contacted by them, and for some time, I continued to think of them as interplanetary invaders. It was probably about a year later that I started to think of them as interdimensional Earth beings, rather than astronauts from another planet. That year I visited the alien dimension many times, and my understanding of them evolved rapidly.

It was nearly two years after that first encounter before it occurred to me that I might have important information about the link between humans and aliens, which might be helpful to others. This awareness triggered my process of discovery—my search for corroboration and information. During this period, I tried to read books about aliens, and I thumbed through magazines about UFO sightings and alien abductions. I forced myself to watch *Communion*. But I didn't find much. "One person's trash is another's treasure," I told myself one day, as I put a popular book aside.

Compared to well-known investigators who had devoted a lifetime to the search, I was a new student. But I was discouraged by their inability to provide helpful information, or even to agree on the most basic questions. The writings of the scientifically oriented researchers bored me. I needed practical help with my experiences, and it often felt as if they were just planting theoretical seeds and hoping that something would grow. I found that the most helpful, compelling, and convincing information came from those who had actually witnessed sightings, or experienced contacts with alien beings.

I'm not an alien-abduction researcher, and I don't plan to become one—I'm simply an individual who was forced into investigating interdimensional reality. But I have concluded that my experiential information may be as valuable as the research of the prominent investigators who study UFO sightings and human-alien contacts.

My abduction experiences and my search for answers have liberated me from my old belief systems. I now believe that human scientists will eventually prove the existence of life on other planets and participate in interplanetary travel. I believe that the Earth has been visited by life forms from other planets, and that humans have been contacted by extraterrestrial beings. But I also believe that this planet is inhabited by interdimensional beings who are studying and altering life on this planet, just as we are—and that their intelligence may be the real driving force behind human technical and scientific progress.

Countless investigators have tried to solve the mystery of UFOs and alien abductions. Some apply the scientific method; others question its relevance to these phenomena. Some attribute alien sightings and contacts to demons and spirits; others deny the existence of such beings. Some use hypnosis as a tool for accessing memories of alien encounters; others say that these states encourage a sense of hysteria. Some believe that the government is withholding information about alien beings; others say it's simply trying to cover its own ignorance on the subject.

Thus, the public hears only confusion: contradictory claims and counterclaims. How can people accept the existence of alien beings when even the most prominent investigators can't reach a consensus? At times, the coverage of UFOs and alien abductions actually feels like a disinformation campaign. As far as I know, no investigator has been able to provide verifiable evidence of the existence of alien beings. Considering the wide diversity of opinion among our alien-abduction researchers, I think it's time to start over.

Well-meaning researchers may be frustrated by their inability to solve the mystery of aliens, but they're pressured to write and speak, to hold their position in the spotlight. Perhaps that's why most discussions about aliens remain focused on dramatic sightings of alien spaceships or UFOs. But perhaps our researchers aren't looking in the right place, or asking the right questions—because I've found that far more interesting information is coming from our direct interactions with alien beings.

Most UFO and alien-abduction researchers seem to be polarized into one of two major camps. Some prefer to use scientific methods; others rely on hypnosis, psychic insights, or other paranormal techniques. But what if our researchers are trying to investigate superior researchers? If we really are experimental subjects, our brains may simply not be capable of understanding the scope and purpose of alien interactions with humans. But it's possible that important information may be accessible to us, stored in our body or our subconscious mind.

The first question we must address seems to be: Are we trying to investigate extraterrestrial beings, interdimensional beings, or both? Extraterrestrial travelers may visit our planet—but as far as I know, I haven't met one yet. For one thing, my neighbors would have complained about the frequent landings on my lawn. Further, the distance between Earth and other potential planetary systems makes this unrealistic, in light of the number of alleged alien abductions. I suspect that extraterrestrial visitations are rare.

On the other hand, I've had many contacts with interdimensional beings who seem to be quite well established on our planet. They've taken me to their subterranean facilities and allowed me to glimpse their world. Because of these experiences, I believe that interdimensional beings maintain a complex web of relationships with humans.

Whether these beings are extraterrestrial or interdimensional, very little, if any, physical evidence of their visitations has been found, and the evidence that does exist has produced very little information. On the other hand, human encounters with alien beings seem to be recorded in the bodies and subconscious minds of the contactees. This would mean that hypnotherapy and paranormal techniques could be quite effective ways to retrieve information about alien contacts.

Another important question is: Can we use the scientific method to produce valid information about aliens? The scientific method is a systematic pursuit of knowledge, based on the application of human logic. However, human logic may not be an effective way of understanding the aliens' superior intelligence and technology. And how can we analyze beings who can transcend time, matter, and reality? We can't summon them to appear and communicate with us. We can't conduct controlled experiments with them. Occasionally they may leave marks or wounds on our bodies, but as far as I know, they never leave physical objects in our dimension.

Another problem is that the scientific approach is based on the researcher's ability to control all variables. Yet aliens routinely distract and deceive us by creating illusions, such as spaceships—and they can control our thoughts, perceptions, and emotions in irresistible ways. When they contact us, we perceive only what they want us to perceive, and believe what only they want us to believe. Since alien-abduction researchers are controlled, rather than in control, the scientific approach is unlikely to ever produce significant information. Interdimensional beings who can transcend time and transform matter can easily evade such an approach.

Despite their inability to reach a consensus, alien-abduction researchers have made one important contribution. They've led us to ask the question: "Who are we?" I believe that this is the question that will eventually produce the right answers for future researchers. Rather than attempting to investigate aliens whom we can't control, our research efforts should be focused on ourselves, on exploring the evidence held in our bodies and subconscious minds.

Some alien-abduction investigators have stressed that hypnosis is not a reliable research method. Their major objection is that the information produced under hypnosis is not factual, and shouldn't be taken at face value. I disagree with them. In the hands of an honest, capable, and knowledgeable hypnotherapist, hypnosis can be a powerful method for discovering information stored in the subconscious mind.

My regressions have convinced me that the subconscious mind is a tremendous repository of information, in which all my memories of alien contacts are readily available for retrieval. However, it is true that retrieving valid information about alien abductions under hypnosis requires us to first work through layers of repressed memories and alien programming.

At first, I was overwhelmed by the sheer volume of it all, but Barbara encouraged me to think of hypnotic exploration as a light, shallow-trance learning experience. "You'll have to go into progressively deeper states of hypnosis to fully explore your alien encounters," she explained. Although I learned a lot from my first regression, I can understand why some researchers maintain that a single regression might not contribute much to our knowledge of alien beings. How can a person relive the significant events of a lifetime in a few hours?

Conscious memory fragments of contactees can also be valuable. Those who retain fragmented memories of their encounters with aliens, whether positive or negative, are probably in their awakening phase. That is, alien scientists are prompting them to understand their hybrid identity. In fact, I can't think of any other reason people would be allowed to retain conscious memories of their alien encounters. Studies of such cases are more likely to produce valid and reliable findings if researchers develop long-term investigative relationships with abductees. Those who have been contacted by alien beings once are likely to have multiple encounters, and will probably continue to receive checkups and adjustments.

Studies of these contactees should include far more than the documentation and analysis of their hypnotic regressions. To substantiate these cases, researchers need to document all the contactee's life experiences—and, once gathered, this information can be compared to a control group. Barbara's research reveals significant life patterns among contactees. For example, most of the abductees she has interviewed were sexually molested before puberty. We need to discover other patterns, document them, and learn from them.

Dreams may also be important sources of information. The documentation and analysis of dreams may lead us to important clues about aliens. Most of my abductions occurred while I was asleep, but I usually retained enough conscious memory of the dreamlike episodes to tell me that aliens had been present. Often I found unusual marks on my body when I awoke, including straight lines arranged in patterns, triangular marks formed with dots, and circular or oval-shaped burn marks.

Another resource is the paranormal approach; psychic phenomena and trance channeling, for example, may be productive ways to learn more about aliens. Some researchers have denounced these methods, and questioned the credibility of information produced by paranormal methods. However, since the "paranormal" is by definition that which can't be explained by science, it's unlikely that such methods could ever be validated to the satisfaction of a trained scientist. Based on my personal experience, however, I would encourage people to learn more about paranormal methods, rather than denouncing them out of hand.

On this topic, it's interesting to note that many abductees demonstrate heightened psychic sensitivity after their alien encounters. I believe that most human hybrids are "psychic," as we define it, because of the communication devices that have been implanted in their bodies. If this is true, psychic ability may simply be an alien technology, rather than a mysterious supernatural force. It's also possible that hybrids retain interdimensional connections that facilitate an expanded state of consciousness.

Trance channeling should also be evaluated objectively. I suspect that it may be a normal function of the human-hybrid brain, rather than a "paranormal" phenomenon. If daydreaming is considered a light state of self-hypnosis, trance channeling may simply be a deeper state of self-hypnosis. Channelers may retrieve information from implants or from the subconscious mind—or they may be communicating with their interdimensional bodies. These theories diminish the mystique of "trance channeling" and redefine it as a human-hybrid function that involves transporting our awareness to past, future, or interdimensional events. Sensory perception in such a deep state can be very vivid, and if the channeler fails to grasp their ability to communicate with their interdimensional self, they may associate it with an external entity.

It's true that aliens could release either deceptive or truthful information—or both—through a psychic or channeler, and their objectives are unknown to us. Therefore, I don't recommend unquestioned belief in everything produced by psychics and channelers. But as the public becomes more accepting of paranormal phenomena, psychics and trance channelers are becoming more prevalent. Are they advanced human hybrids? Are their brains unique in some way? Are they programmed with special communication abilities? If so, we need to learn more about their potential to retrieve information about alien beings.

I also have ideas of how some people are attracted to UFO and alien-abduction research in the first place. Some of them may be human hybrids who are struggling to crack their human shells. Either innate or programmed knowledge of their alien heritage is driving them to discover their interdimensional connections and complete their alien-programmed missions.

Most of the researchers I've met claim to have had some form of contact with alien intelligence, and I've wondered if they share a common programming. Were they created and programmed to educate the rest of us about alien beings? Do they fit the "batch consignment theory?" Whether researchers agree or disagree among themselves, their studies force us to think about the existence of other beings, and seem to be facilitating our gradual acceptance of aliens.

Of course, aliens may be orchestrating this process and feeding information to researchers on their own schedule, not ours. For example, I believe that aliens directed me to write this book, and fed certain thoughts and ideas into my mind. Therefore, I assume that they want me to present my information and theories to the public at this time.

I remember one evening when Barbara and I sat in front of her fireplace and she reflected on her work as an alien-abduction researcher. I asked her why she was doing all this research. She replied, "I don't know. I don't know of any other investigator who's compiled a comparable volume of information about alien abductions. And sometimes I wonder why they allow me to do this work. I want to help people gain their freedom, instead of thinking that they are controlled by aliens."

I said, "Barbara, the old infrastructure of our knowledge is crumbling. Your alien-abduction research is contributing to that deterioration, and helping to create new information about human life. The aliens haven't stopped you—they must approve of your efforts, and maybe they're even guiding you."

Barbara gazed into the flickering fire and replied, "You know, I sometimes think of myself as a human rights activist, rather than a researcher. I devoted myself to learning about alien beings more than ten years ago, but my real commitment has been to people. I've spent all these years trying to figure out how to protect our human rights."

Barbara's desire to be of service touched my heart. She had certainly helped me regain control of my life—I was happy, free, and productive again. I said, "You've helped countless people recover their freedom. I didn't start to heal until you helped me discover my interdimensional heritage." I had a momentary image of Barbara as a caring nurse, quietly and gently awakening people to a new and unfamiliar world. "But do the aliens understand our concept of human rights, or is this just more of our frail human logic?"

"They seem to be controlling human evolution, and our relationship with them seems to be evolving."

"You may be right, Barbara. You know, I wonder if the current relationship between humans and aliens may be analogous to the abolition of the slavery in America. Freedom arises when people accept others, rather than being afraid of them, or trying to control them. We may be learning to accept a technologically advanced interdimensional race, and the aliens may be trying to transform us into compatible neighbors. Perhaps humans and aliens will become more alike as time passes, and our two dimensions become increasingly integrated.

"The aliens want you to continue your research, and they've provided most of the information for my book. They seem to be orchestrating a worldwide human awakening. We need to strip away our old thinking about them and begin to look for answers within—just as my search for answers turned into an inner journey."

"Most of your information about aliens was recorded in your own brain," Barbara said.

"Yes, and we absorb even more information about alien beings during each of our contacts. Our journeys to their dimension are recorded within us, and they are now allowing us to discover this information. I believe that the aliens are getting ready to reveal who they are. But first, they're helping us discover who *we* are."

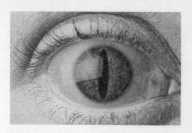

Part Three

11 | MY ALIEN EMERGES, FEET FIRST

DOCUMENTING INFORMATION about aliens is like walking a tightrope without a net. One must be able to swiftly change positions and viewpoints. Like an acrobat, I place myself in a precarious situation each time I express a new theory about the relationship between humans and aliens.

When I mention my interdimensional journeys, I always feel apprehensive and wonder how people will react. However, the aliens have taught me that the remainder of my life is likely to be a series of uncertain, unsteady steps. I'm never certain about anything about aliens—and when I do have clear insights, they simply inspire more unanswerable questions. However, I started writing with a strong sense that the aliens had deposited all the information I would need in my mind. "The book will evolve," I assured myself as I began the process.

Aliens may be programming human hybrids like myself to learn through self-discovery and self-acceptance, and we are likely to learn more about them as we discover ourselves. Important information about them may be archived in our minds or implanted in our bodies. To retrieve the information, we must learn to express the interdimensional aspects of our being. In other words, we must integrate our human and interdimensional selves, and learn to function in both worlds. I believe this is how we will eventually establish two-way communication with our alien creators, and learn to co-exist with them.

The idea of integrating with an invisible alien world may seem far-fetched, but it appears that alien beings have already initiated the process. In recent years, reports of alien contacts and abductions have increased significantly, and each human contact with aliens can bring our worlds a bit closer together, if we retrieve and study the records of these contacts. Our subconscious minds may be our ports of entry into an interdimensional reality.

My understanding of all this began about a year and a half after my first alien visitation. I was agitated and having difficulty maintaining my will to live. It felt as if part of me was in another dimension, and the rest of me wanted to be there, too. On my next visit to Barbara, I said, "I have to find the source of these troubling feelings. I'm having disturbing dreams and thoughts, and I'm preoccupied with a desire to be in the alien dimension, instead of here."

My desire to escape physical life disturbed Barbara. She suggested, "Let's put you into hypnosis and take a look at your recent contacts and journeys."

Once I was resting comfortably, Barbara suggested, "Go back in time. Go back to discover the source of your frustrations."

I immediately became distressed, and Barbara asked me what I was experiencing. We were both surprised by my response.

"I don't live in the physical world all of the time." After a pause, I continued, "I just saw myself walking in an arid, uninviting, unfamiliar place. I'm walking on sand and rocks the color of red clay, and surrounded by large boulders of the same color."

Barbara asked me if I could identify the area, but I could not. "It's not near home." I wondered if it was even on this planet. At this point, I went deeper and received a clearer image. I said, "I've traveled to this place many times; a part of me knows exactly where I am. But I need to go deep below the surface. I'll be safe there."

With those words, part of me left Barbara's control. My thoughts were far distant from my physical body. I felt uncomfortable and frightened. I seemed to be in a dimension halfway between the Earth and somewhere else.

"What are you feeling?" Barbara asked.

"I'm like a young bird just kicked out of its nest. I'm somewhere between dimensions and may not be able to get to my destination while part of me is conscious." My body was now throbbing with anxiety. Something extraordinary was happening, and I wasn't sure that my conscious mind could handle the experience.

Barbara was trying to control my experience through hypnosis, but she had no influence over the part of me that had left my body. I was distressed; my body was trembling. I had never experienced the interdimensional place 'consciously', and was like an astronaut who just arrived on a newly discovered planet. I didn't know what to expect.

Barbara began to speak, and I tried to focus on the sound of her voice. "You saw yourself walking in an arid place. Please stop what you are doing and look at yourself as you appear there. Describe your appearance to me."

"I can only see my feet and legs. I don't want to see the rest of my body."

"Why are you reacting so strongly to seeing your feet and legs?"

"I don't want to look! I'm afraid to look at them again!"

"Please relax and be calm. You are what you are. Don't be afraid."

I was still trembling in terror, and refused to accept Barbara's repeated suggestions to describe my body. Although in a deep hypnotic state, I felt numb and couldn't speak. I did not understand the significance of looking at my feet and legs, but my reaction was so strong that nearly two years would pass before I could view that startling image again.

"Let's talk about the rocky place," Barbara said, trying to reestablish our link. "You were walking on the surface."

I said slowly, "Yes. Right now, I'm on the surface; but I must go below. I cannot tolerate being above ground very long. I won't be able to breathe if I don't get to the safe underground area."

"Inhale deeply. Draw air into your lungs. You will be safe."

An unfamiliar voice exclaimed, "I don't use lungs!"

Barbara was surprised by this sharp response, and understood that she was no longer speaking to me. But she continued to maintain our communication link. "How do you breathe?"

My right hand moved to the side of my neck; and, in the deep, strange-sounding voice, I said, "Air passes through these small openings. They're like gills."

There was a long pause. I don't know what Barbara was thinking, but I suspect she needed some time to recover her composure. She had to be wondering who, or what, was speaking to her. The voice was so different from mine, and had an angry, unfriendly tone. Eventually it interrupted the silence.

"We do not need to discuss my appearance."

"Are you feeling uncomfortable?"

"A part of me is there, with you. But this part of me is very anxious to get below, where I can breathe comfortably."

My physical distress was obvious to Barbara; she was becoming concerned about my well-being. "Can you project yourself down? Are others, like you, nearby? If so, do you need to be with them?"

"Oh! Help me!" I screamed in agony. My normal voice had returned, but I was gasping for air.

"Tell me, Jim, how do you feel?" Barbara asked, speaking my name.

"I'm confused, divided. My physical body is with you, but I'm also in another body, and I can't get to the place where I need to be."

"Can you be in two places simultaneously?"

"I am right now! I'm in two different bodies. I'm in two different dimensions!" I was shouting at her.

Barbara maintained her self-control, and instructed me to breathe deeply and relax. "If you become too uncomfortable in your interdimensional form, you can return to your physical body. But if you can continue to function in both worlds, we have an excellent opportunity to learn more about your total being."

I focused on her words, imagining them as helpful hands reaching out to rescue me, and tried to calm myself.

"While you're in your other body, I'd like to ask you some questions. Can you answer me?"

Her voice was my lifeline; I wanted her to keep talking.

"If you're a human hybrid being, why are you in human form?"

"I'm not in human life by choice. I was forced to participate in the reproductive program. That's why I've been in a human body."

"Why are aliens populating this planet with human hybrid beings?"

"This is a very small planet. Its main attractions are water and vegetation, which produce valuable energies and resources. My ancestors arrived here at least ten thousand years ago, and their race is still adapting to its environment. Also, my ancestors weren't very beautiful. The hybridization of humans with my ancestral race is creating a more beautiful species, or race; and it's facilitating our adaptation to the Earth's atmosphere."

"Will others of your ancestral species be able to live here like you do?"

Although both of my bodies were distressed, I was still functioning in two dimensions. I was clinging to the sound of Barbara's voice, but fast approaching my panic threshold—if I didn't reach the underground destination soon, I expected to die. My lungs felt as if they were collapsing, and I was gasping for air. I shouted, "Somebody has to let me in. Please, let me in!"

Barbara told me to project myself to my destination. "Follow your usual way of entering the underground area. You've traveled back and forth before, haven't you?"

Yes, I had traveled here before. "But I don't know how to do this at will," I said. "I've never tried to travel here while I was active in the conscious world. I have to know how to maintain my human body while I'm in this dimension."

"Are you usually assisted by alien beings when you travel to this dimension?"

"Yes. I think so." Then I hesitated. "I've never thought about it before." The aliens had always facilitated my movement between dimensions, and my conscious mind had never questioned their methods.

"Focus on your previous journeys, and maybe you'll slide through."

I tried to follow her suggestion, but nothing happened. She asked me to find out how aliens conveyed me to their dimension. But I was feeling claustrophobic and couldn't respond. The stress was too great. Instead, I exclaimed, "I see figures approaching. They're not human!" Abruptly, my human body stopped trembling, and my breathing returned to normal.

Did an alien rescue team send me back to my human body? I don't know what happened, but I burst completely out of the deep hypnotic trance. I opened my eyes and looked at Barbara. Her face was a beautiful sight, and I was thrilled to be back in her office.

I said, "I need to learn to travel interdimensionally. I want to enter the underground facility, where I was trying to go."

She asked me to share my thoughts about the other dimension. I was sure that part of me had traveled to another world, but I couldn't understand why I wasn't allowed to enter the safe place. Some part of me must have known the answer, but my conscious mind was stymied.

"I wasn't permitted to enter. I didn't get in." I was disappointed. I had gone to the right location, but hadn't gained entrance. It seemed that I couldn't enter the alien facility while conscious. "Maybe I couldn't have tolerated a prolonged simultaneous awareness of two dimensions."

I closed my eyes, and Barbara allowed me to drift. I was tired and needed to rest. I assumed that the session was over, and was thinking how wonderful it was just to lie there in Barbara's office. Then I heard her soft voice say, "You just glimpsed the arid, rocky place. Now you'll be able to look at it without anxiety. Look at it now as if you're watching a movie screen, and you'll understand more."

I was back under hypnosis again, but instead of following her suggestion, I said, "I'm controlled by some kind of signal." I felt such a desperate need to speak that I started shouting again. "I need to say something! I receive messages from aliens through their signals. The signals are used to take me places. I've done most of my work for the aliens as a result of receiving messages through their signals."

The aliens have called, or signalled, me many times. I don't know what happens when they signal me while I'm asleep. My conscious mind may deny these calls and treat them as dreams; but when I wake up after these calls, I have memory fragments, emotional residue, or physical discomfort. These are clues that the aliens have been present.

I remember more about my alien contacts when they signal or transport me while I'm conscious. If I hear signals while I'm active, I become very drowsy, as if drugged. Several times, the messages have instructed me to lie down. If I resist, the drowsiness and the messages intensify until I can no longer function. A few times I've received signals at work, and have had to leave the office and go home. I had heard the same signals the afternoon that I developed the high fever and had to be hospitalized.

Barbara guided me deeper and asked me to learn more about the signals.

"I can't avoid them. They overpower my brain and anesthetize my mind."

"How are they used to transport you?"

"When I'm transported without my physical body, my thoughts drift into the signal, and I lose awareness of my surroundings. Then my other body arrives at the destination from which the signal is projected."

Wondering how the signals function, I imagined an alien operator in front of a gigantic control panel. As colored lights blinked, the alien transmitted signal beams to human hybrids around the world. The beams delivered instructions to the implants in their bodies, which in turn relayed instructions to their brain—and the hybrids would respond like robots.

"Business as usual," I thought aloud.

"What?"

"Imagine a caveman walking into his cave and finding a TV set, tuned to *Star Trek*. He would be as puzzled as I am, trying to explain the alien signal system."

"You're doing a great job. Please organize your thoughts and share them with me."

Although I had received alien signals so many times, I didn't understand the technology well enough to describe it. I could describe my perceptions. "At times the aliens have taken my entire being, my human body and my essence. But they only take my other body when the abductions are initiated by a signal."

"I asked you to look at a movie screen before. Please look at it now."

On the screen I saw my early abductions. The first time, when the alien removed me from my bed and transported me to the underground laboratory, I remembered feeling as if I had two bodies. "One was physical, and it remained on the bed. The body on the examining table had all my human senses, but no physical properties. The alien entered my bedroom to prepare my physical body for the abduction. I couldn't be transported while my body was at its normal temperature."

Barbara encouraged me to say more, but what I was going to say didn't seem plausible. "Before transforming my molecular structure, the alien reduced my body temperature. I think my physical body was just about frozen before my other body was conveyed to the alien laboratory."

"How was this abduction different from any before?" I wondered out loud. The inner voice promptly replied, "You participated! This abduction was a learning experience. When the teacher chilled and prepared your human body for the transportation of your interdimensional body, you were conscious. Your limited awareness perceived the teacher as an enemy, but it was simply teaching you how to disengage from your human body."

What a totally new perspective. I never suspected that I was a willing student of interdimensional travel that first night.

Barbara asked me to replay the movie. "Watch the movie as many times as necessary. Gain as much understanding of this experience as possible."

As I replayed the scenes, my human body felt heavy and awkward, and I began to think of it as a temporary aspect of my being. "My other body, the one the alien delivered to the examination table, must be my permanent body."

"That's a very important idea. Tell me about your other body."

I didn't want to say it. I had to pause and inhale deeply first. "My permanent body looks like the aliens, and it lives in both dimensions!"

With these words, I finally penetrated to the core of the issue that had been haunting me. I was so busy processing this thought that I lost track of Barbara's voice. I continued, "It's my permanent body, and it will live beyond my human lifetime. When my human life ends, my alien body will return to the other dimension."

When Barbara snapped her fingers at the count of three to end the regression, I didn't feel refreshed, as I usually did. The idea of my interdimensional body felt overwhelming; I wanted to deny everything that had happened in the regression. I told myself that this time my imagination had gone too far. I couldn't share it with Barbara, but I felt deep disappointment with myself.

As I turned out of her driveway, I was overcome by loneliness. *No one will understand me. No one will believe me. I'm all alone in the world.* I longed to escape my human body and dwell in the other world. I made the familiar turn onto the highway on autopilot, completely unaware of my surroundings. My imagination had really overdone it this time. *How could you journey to another world? How could you experience two dimensions simultaneously?* I demanded.

During this disturbing hypnotic session, my interdimensional self emerged, feet first—but I was too frightened to look at my interdimensional body. The scaly reptilian feet and bony legs were a shocking sight, and my conscious mind wasn't ready to see the rest of it. It was nothing like the slender alien who had left my human body during the first regression.

Nearly two years passed before I read the transcript of this regression, and even then I had difficulty with some of it. It wasn't until I read all the transcripts in chronological order that I finally understood how this session fit into my self-discovery process and my acceptance of my alien heritage.

The sight of my interdimensional feet and legs forced me to take another important step toward integrating the interdimensional aspects of my hybrid being. After this, I could finally ask myself, "Was the 'alien' who left my body during the first regression simply one of my interdimensional forms?"

12 | SOMETHING'S HAPPENING, BARBARA!

HI, BARBARA. Something important is happening!"

It was a year and a half after my interdimensional regression. I knew I'd been traveling interdimensionally in my sleep, but I didn't know if I was being escorted by alien beings, or if I was traveling on my own. For weeks, I'd been asking the aliens to take me back to the underground lab and show me their complete operation. Each night before falling asleep, I would state my request out loud. I was still searching for evidence to verify my theories, and I wanted them to show me specific areas of their human engineering facilities so I could describe them in this book.

When I started my routine of asking to be taken to their dimension, I felt confident that I could accept whatever they were willing to reveal. By this time, I was well into the writing and feeling confident. I just wanted concrete evidence of their existence. But after a few weeks of this, I began to feel tired and confused. Fragmented memories of alien contacts were piling up in my conscious mind, and I couldn't piece them together.

My opening remark was enough to send Barbara scrambling for her tape recorder. "Please hold your thoughts while I get set up. I must record this." Barbara always seemed to know when I was about to tell her about interesting alien contacts. I heard her mutter, "Jim Walden, Telephone Conversations," as she inserted a familiar tape. Then I heard excerpts of my voice, from previous conversations, as she searched for the end of the tape.

My thoughts drifted, and I started to make a mental inventory of the memory fragments that I wanted to discuss with her. There were several, but one stood out; it involved an interdimensional journey to a small farm.

I was very familiar with the scene. My grandparents had lived and worked on the farm for nearly sixty years, and many of my favorite childhood memories took place there. I was always thrilled to be allowed to stay with my grandparents, and more than willing to do chores, like feeding the animals or pulling weeds in their bountiful garden.

The farm was peaceful, quiet, and insulated from the rest of the world. To me, it was an enchanted place. Deep forests surrounded the farmhouse, the crop fields, and the hay meadows, providing an endless playground for me. When I went into the woods alone to pick huckleberries, I sometimes looked over my shoulders and strained for a glimpse of the "little people." Now and then I had heard the grown-ups talk about them, and I wanted to meet the elusive beings.

My grandfather passed away in 1979, and two years later my grandmother sold the farm. I was sorry to see it leave the family, but I was busy with graduate school and my career—and George, the new owner, seemed to love the farm as much as I did. He had lived his entire life in Detroit,

Michigan, and had dreamed of living on a small farm in the Ozarks, growing fresh food and beautiful flowers.

But George never moved to the farm. Just after buying it he became ill; he rented it out for a few years, hoped that his health would improve, and visited when he could. However, neither George's health nor the farm improved. As rental property, the old house and the fields deteriorated rapidly.

I was surprised when George called in May 1986 and asked, "Would you like the farm?" He proposed a trade. "I'll give you the farm in exchange for your new log home on Table Rock Lake. I'd like to spend my remaining days watching the lake from your front porch." I asked about his dream of living on a farm, and he said he would never be strong enough to grow a garden. "The farm needs you," he said. "You're the only one who will care for it as lovingly as your grandparents did." Of course, I accepted his offer.

By that fall, the house was fully restored, and the fields were cleared, mowed, and occupied by beautiful horses. I often thought that my grandfather would be proud of me for restoring the farm's dignity. For the next five years I spent my weekends and summers at the farm. I would become lost in time there. Other people loved it, too, and many people consulted me there for psychic readings and attended group healing sessions, which I facilitated.

Five years later, I sold the farm to a happy young family. My new job as a city administrator consumed most of my time and energy, and I could no longer maintain the large garden and keep the farm looking pretty. The family fell in love with the house, the fields, and the woods on their first visit. They talked about cows, chickens, and living there for the rest of their lives. I was glad to sell it to them.

"Okay." Barbara's voice interrupted my reverie. "Please state the date. I want to be sure we're recording."

"Sunday, March 5, 1995."

"Okay, we're recording. What's happening, Jim?"

"I don't know where some of my recent dream encounters begin or end. I only remember isolated segments. But I am experiencing all of the familiar side effects of contacts with aliens.

Barbara knew that by "side effects" I meant I was feeling tired, confused, and frustrated.

"I've been asking the aliens to take me to their underground facilities."

I knew this would surprise and alarm her, so I quickly kept talking. "I want to know the truth about their human processing operations before I finish the manuscript. During one of my abductions they showed me decapitated bodies and severed limbs, and I've never understood why. I've had several encounters during the past two or three weeks, and I'm emotionally exhausted."

Before this, Barbara and I had never discussed the human "processing facilities," as I called them. However, I knew that many abductees had reported frightening trips to subterranean facilities, where they had seen gruesome sights of dismembered human bodies. Some abductees were convinced that aliens consume humans as nourishment. I just wanted to know the truth.

I could hear the concern in Barbara's voice as she asked me to go on. "What do you remember about your encounters?"

"I don't seem to have a lot of clear information. I seem to be collecting some important information, but I think you'll have to extract it from my subconscious."

Barbara understood. "You mean you'll have to go into hypnosis to understand what's been happening and retrieve the information you want." She asked me to tell her more about my dream encounters.

"Friday night or early Saturday, I dreamt of the farm where I used to live. I don't remember why I was there, or what happened. I remember standing in front of the house and looking toward a large pond on the opposite ridge. A narrow valley separates the house and the pond. Near the pond I saw something unusual; it looked like a huge television."

"Can you describe it in more detail?"

"It looked like a gigantic television screen with tentacles, or antennae, attached to it. I don't know if I went into it. I remember looking at it from a distance, but when I try to see it more closely, the memory fades. I couldn't figure out why such a strange-looking object would be sitting in a pasture."

"Can you remember anything else?"

"Yes, I had a conversation with someone. They explained that aliens are attracted to the area because of the spring water." I was referring to the local springs that had been giving water since the land had been settled. "It seems that aliens require a supply of pure water."

"You may be right."

"I've never thought about it before," I said, wondering what they needed water for.

"Yes," Barbara said. "Many sightings have been documented over lakes and ponds. I don't know what the connection is, but many farmers have seen crafts over their ponds."

"I still have a mental image of this large thing. From a distance, I wondered if it could be the doorway to an alien facility. But when I looked directly at it, it just looked like a huge television screen."

Barbara asked if I knew why it was in the pasture. "No. It was just sitting there, near the pond. At first, I assumed that it had landed there, but after thinking about it all day yesterday, I'm not sure. It may be there all of the time, but invisible to human eyes. Could it be the portal to an underground facility?"

My alien contacts and interdimensional journeys have taught me to question everything. Things may not be what they seem to be. "It didn't look like a spaceship, but for some reason, this image caused me to wonder if aliens had been established in the area for a long time."

"Did you have any contacts with aliens while you lived on the farm?"

"No. I don't have any conscious memories of alien contacts while I lived there. I never even thought about aliens until the year after I sold the farm."

"Was the object in the water or on the side of the pond?"

"It was near the side of the pond. It was just sitting in a clearing on the ridge, next to the pond." Suddenly I remembered that I had awoken from this dream with painful leg cramps; I told Barbara how the muscles in the back of my legs had turned into hard, painful knots.

"All day Saturday, I felt out of sorts, and my legs were sore from the cramps. I was emotionally disturbed, without knowing why, and I wanted to get away from my house. So I went out of town for the day with some friends. We went to an outlet mall, where I was able to escape my disturbed thoughts for a few hours."

Barbara asked if I felt better after leaving home.

"The drowsiness and the signals intensified all day; and by late evening, I had difficulty staying awake. I went to bed at ten, abandoned my resistance, and asked the aliens to take me underground."

"How do you feel this morning?"

"Almost helpless. I couldn't get out of bed until after noon; I think something major must have happened during the night."

"Did you feel drugged?"

"Definitely. I'm still in a stupor. My mind isn't functioning, and I can't control my psychomotor skills."

"Do you remember any dreams from last night?"

"Yes. I was naked, and I was very embarrassed about it."

Barbara asked why I was naked, but I didn't know. Then she asked, "Where were you?"

"I was in a tank, or a pond, filled with a slightly congealed blue liquid. It looked and felt like half-set gelatin. I had some type of hose in my mouth, but I don't know why. This encounter must be very significant." I remembered blowing through the hose, rather than breathing through it. "I don't understand any of this."

"What position were you in—vertical or horizontal?"

"At first I moved around the tank, but eventually, I sank into the blue liquid. I have no idea where I went, or what happened after that."

"How big was the tank? Could you swim in it?"

"No. It wasn't large enough for swimming. It was the size of a very large stock tank; and it seemed to be oval-shaped."

"Now, try to remember—do you have any other memories of this experience?"

"Yes!" Her question suddenly brought more fragments to the surface. "I do. Later, I was near some muddy, flowing water, and I walked into a narrow valley surrounded by steep hills. I looked ahead and sensed that people had lived in the valley a long time ago. I didn't want to go farther into the valley. I wanted to leave immediately."

"What did you do?"

"I turned around and started to leave; but as I turned, two men came toward me. Their faces looked human, so I extended my hand to greet them. But they couldn't shake hands like we do; their fingers were curled and they couldn't straighten them out."

"Were their fingers curled under?"

"Curled under? Yes, and their skin was rough. Their hands had a rough texture."

"Please, Jim, continue your description. We need to document all possible information about these beings."

I could now remember it all clearly. One of them looked old; the other was younger. "They were wearing disguises; they looked like hill people."

"They looked like scruffy hill people?"

"Yes. They looked shabby. One of them asked me if I was related to my father, who's dead. I told them I was, and we started talking about him. That's my last clear memory of the encounter."

"Your last memory involves discussing your father with the two men?"

"I can't recall anything else. But our talk has restored my consciousness. My mind is clearing."

"What does your inner voice say about these memories? Have you acquired any new information about the aliens or their facilities?"

"I've been asking the aliens to show me their facilities and reveal more information. I know I am assuming some risks. If I'm taken underground, I don't have any guarantee of my safety. But I thought that the aliens wanted me to finish the book and that they wanted me to find some more information to include in the book."

Barbara didn't respond, and I hoped she was agreeing with me. "I feel as if I've been used like a fisherman's net. I've swept through these encounters and loaded up with information. My brain is full, and I can't maintain my balance with this information overload."

"What should we do?"

"I guess I should come to see you and let you empty the net."

Barbara agreed. I needed another hypnotic regression. The fragments of my recent encounters indicated that I might be able to retrieve some new information about the alien beings and their facilities. We decided to meet at her house the following weekend.

Before hanging up, Barbara added, "Leg cramps may be an abduction clue. According to my research, they are an aftereffect of alien contacts. Leg cramps result from temporary potassium depletion, which occurs during interdimensional encounters. I've documented it many times."

After I promised to eat more bananas, she added, "Please monitor your blood pressure after an encounter, too. Blood pressure fluctuations are another side effect of alien interference."

After talking with Barbara, I felt much better. I was excited about the weekend, and anxious to unload my subconscious and explore my recent encounters. Also, I had the uncanny feeling that I would discover more about my interdimensional self this time.

While shaving the next morning, I looked at my mustache and thought aloud, "I'm tired of trimming you." The razor seemed to take over, and my mustache fell into the toilet. As I saw my pale upper lip for the first time in more than twenty-five years, I felt naked.

13 | OLD BIG HEAD SHOWS UP

KYLE AND I left the office early Friday afternoon, and arrived just as the sun slipped below the western sky. Hugs and warm greetings from Barbara and Tim, her husband, made the long trip feel worthwhile. "You look happy and healthy," Barbara said.

"Yes, I'm feeling well. And I'm happy to see you. I probably wouldn't be alive today if Jane hadn't given me your name."

Barbara and Tim were enjoying happy, productive years. Tim was writing a novel; Barbara's research was fascinating, and her enthusiasm inspiring. I settled into a comfortable chair near the wood stove, and recalled my first visit, three years earlier. "When I sat in this chair the first time, my eyes were red and swollen from crying. I was a victim then, and expecting to be killed by aliens any day. Now my eyes are my portals to an interdimensional world that few humans have glimpsed—and this time, I'm here to learn more about that world."

When Barbara has something disturbing on her mind, she develops certain nervous mannerisms: she smiles and repeatedly swallows and clears her throat; she wrings her hands and paces the room, pretending to look for something. She started doing all that now, and I asked her what was on her mind. She said, "I might as well tell you. Jane had an encounter Wednesday night, and she thinks you were with the aliens."

This didn't come as a complete surprise; we'd heard similar accounts before. An Iowa woman who was abducted from a farmhouse in 1992 was the first to report seeing me during an abduction. In addition to the aliens, she said, a human man, matching my description, was present when she was abducted. When the woman described me and the interior features of my house in convincing detail, Barbara became alarmed. She prepared a video lineup of male faces, and asked the woman to identify the one who'd been with the aliens during her abduction. The woman selected my image immediately.

Next, a man in Louisiana reported a similar encounter. Over the next few months, the list of "Jim" sightings continued to grow. I had no idea why people were seeing my face during their abductions. The aliens seemed to be using my image, and I was deeply concerned and confused by it.

Barbara continued, still nervous. "There's more. I noticed something different when you arrived. Your mustache is gone."

"I shaved it off last week," I said, wondering why that would upset her.

"Exactly when did you shave it off?"

"Monday morning. I don't know why. I just looked at it, and impulsively decided to cut it off. I was tired of trimming it every morning. I've had it for twenty-five years, you know."

Barbara said, "Jane's been sick every morning since her encounter. It's a peculiar form of morning sickness. During this encounter, she was restrained on a table, covered, and surrounded by light. She saw you standing at the foot of the table, from the waist up; and you were naked!"

"What happened?" I asked, embarrassed.

"I'm not sure."

"If he had a mustache, the naked man couldn't have been me."

Just as I said this, the phone rang. When Barbara said, "Hi, Jane," the rest of us exchanged surprised glances.

After a pause, Barbara said, "Jane, Jim's sitting right here. Please repeat to him what you just said to me." She handed the phone to me.

"What's up, Jane?"

"The man at the foot of the table couldn't have been you. He looked just like you, but he was clean-shaven. He didn't have a mustache." She added that the man wore glasses, while I usually wear contacts. I replied, "I have a new pair of glasses, Jane, and I haven't worn my contacts this week." We were both silent. I didn't tell her that I'd shaved my mustache two days before her encounter.

When I got off the phone, I said, "Jane's report must be an omen; I'm supposed to be here. The aliens seem to have summoned me for this regression. I bet we'll discover some important information tomorrow."

We stayed up talking for another hour or two. We marveled at Jane's ability to remember such accurate details—but we were all rather unnerved by the whole thing. I went to sleep wondering if I was truly participating in alien abductions, or if the aliens were just using my image.

The next morning I asked Barbara, "Have you heard from Jane? Is she feeling better?"

Jane had already called to report that she was feeling much better. Barbara added, "If she's up to it, she'd like to meet with us tomorrow."

Now that my concern about Jane was relieved, I was anxious to explore my interdimensional visit to the old farm. I approached this regression with a casual attitude—all my traumatic experiences with aliens seemed to be in the distant past. Barbara asked Kyle if he'd like to observe, and he eagerly accepted her invitation. We didn't anticipate that anything unusual would happen. The video and recording equipment was set up in Barbara's "summer parlor." I nestled into a pallet of cushions, and entered my familiar hypnotic cloud. Within minutes, I was in hypnosis.

"Please begin when you feel comfortable, Jim."

"I seem to be lost."

"Become comfortable in that void, and when you're ready, move forward."

"I want to discuss my recent experiences at the farm." My mind was filled with unfamiliar thoughts and images, and I spoke slowly. "I see something at the farm; it's a form of intelligence. A radar screen comes to mind—I can't think of a better analogy. It's a large object, which is actually under the ground."

"Study the object carefully, and tell me about it."

"It's a large circular object, deep within the Earth. I saw it in my dream, but then it appeared to be above ground, and it looked like a huge television screen. Also, it now appears much larger than in my dream. It's about sixteen to eighteen feet in diameter." The object was clear in my mind, but difficult to describe.

Barbara asked me to continue.

"It's round and flat on top, and anchored deep in the Earth. On the bottom, it tapers to a point, like a toy top. It may have been in the Earth for a thousand years or more. But it's been modified or changed in some way during the last hundred years. Similar objects are planted in the Earth in other strategic locations. They're located around the globe, like benchmarks—they facilitate the aliens' communications somehow."

With that last comment, the familiar pain struck behind my left ear. As usual, it felt as if someone was kicking the side of my head with a booted foot. I couldn't speak. Barbara let me rest, and the pain slowly subsided.

When we resumed, I explained, "I was getting too close—there's something I'm not supposed to divulge about those objects."

I couldn't remember what I'd been saying when the pain struck, but I could still see the strange images. "The aliens use these things to survey surrounding areas and facilitate communication. They're like gigantic brains—receiving, processing, and transmitting information. They're like underground satellites.

"They facilitate interdimensional travel, too. When aliens travel, they maintain their bearings and find their destination with the help of these buried objects, which are located in an intricate network around the globe." I seemed to be struggling to retrieve information buried deep in my brain. It was like seeing a person's face and not being able to remember their name.

"There's a numerical system involved. The Earth's surface is divided into grids. Energies flow along the grid lines, and each grid is designated by a number. To travel, aliens visualize grid numbers—and their bodies are transported to the destination that correlates with those numbers. Sometimes, people see objects in the sky...." With those words, my voice fell silent. I couldn't complete the sentence; my vocal cords were frozen.

Barbara instructed me to move to the next significant event. Although we couldn't safely pursue this topic now, I knew she'd return to it later.

"I'm looking at the Earth from a distance, from outer space, and I can see that we have some inaccurate assumptions about our world." With my interdimensional eyes, I saw a complex network of alien technology criss-crossing the planet—multi-colored, flowing energies covering the entire globe. "I'm seeing the Earth's nervous system. This planet is more than a large ball of matter. It's an intelligent communications system."

I felt an inner conflict, as my human brain tried to process the interdimensional images now flowing into my awareness. Somehow Barbara knew that part of me had left my human body. "You're viewing the planet through your interdimensional eyes, aren't you? Please use those eyes to look at yourself. Which body are you in?"

My voice, gestures, and mannerisms changed abruptly.

"My favorite one, of course."

"What do you mean?"

"I don't get to be in this body often, so I'm really enjoying myself. This is my natural body—and being in it is like stripping off all my masks and costumes. It's the way an actor feels after he leaves the stage, and removes his wig and makeup. In this body, I'm free."

"Look at your form. Tell me what you look like."

The words seemed to come into my consciousness from a far distant mind—and this time, I wasn't afraid to see my interdimensional body. "My feet are long and slender. My toes are long, too—they're at least six inches longer than my human toes. They're not like those ugly human toes I usually wear. They're more pointy, and have more joints—ten or twelve. I don't use them much, but they're really fun."

"Please continue."

"In this body, I have a very flexible skeletal structure. I'm limber and loose. I can move about freely. I like to stretch out and be comfortable."

"What is the most comfortable position for you?"

"I really prefer to be upright. It's the easiest way to move around."

"What does your face look like? Could you describe your head?"

"My head is larger than most," I said proudly. The size of my head seemed to make me special.

"Why is it larger?"

"It's larger because I'm old. So many young ones are being produced now. But I'm really old. I've been around for thousands of years." I really wanted Barbara to appreciate the significance of my age. "We're changing things and producing many new hybrid strains. But I'm *old*. I'd like others to know that."

"Can you tell me about your culture and your species long ago? Please tell me what it was like when you were young."

"When I was young, we controlled everything here on Earth. We were the ultimate authority, and were never rebuked. Now our control has been diminished—we no longer have absolute power. We've diluted our authority by hybridizing our species.

"I'm one of the few who can trace their existence back to a pristine time when humans were a very low life-form. Now we're gradually passing the responsibility for maintaining and preserving this planet on to humans. Contrary to what many of you believe, we're actually relinquishing control of this planet. This is the ultimate result of the human hybridization process. I truly dislike that term, but it's one you can grasp and understand. Personally, I resent the crossbreeding of my species with a lower life form."

I was seething with anger, but Barbara wanted to keep me talking. "Did your species decide to crossbreed with humans?"

"We should rest. I'm very angry, and I prefer to avoid violence."

Barbara asked gently, "Please tell me why you're angry. I'd like to understand your feelings."

"I'll give you an example. In the future, separate human races won't exist; one blended race will inhabit the Earth. This means that interracial relationships are part of human evolution—but some humans would still like to protect the 'purity' of their race.

"I'm speaking as an individual, not as a spokesperson for my species. My species has been diluted by crossbreeding with humans. We're creating an intelligent hybrid race, which will be capable of perpetuating and preserving life on this planet. I understand the process theoretically, but as an individual, I must mourn the loss of my species. Can you understand?"

"Yes. I understand your concerns. But why are you relinquishing control of this planet?"

"Colonization was our original purpose. But now that it has been accomplished, the old ones, like myself, are no longer needed. We've shared our intelligence during the development of the hybrids."

"Tell me how you feel about the hybrids. Are you concerned that they won't be able to handle their responsibilities? Do you see a loss of integrity in them?"

"Here you must understand the sense of supremacy that governs my being. I'm superior because of my intelligence and cumulative experience; the hybrids will never be as capable. When you mix a color with a clear liquid, the color is diluted. That's how I feel about humans—as diluted life forms, their intelligence will never be comparable to the intelligence of my ancestors."

"Then why are you relinquishing control of the planet to them?"

"A specific answer to your question is impossible. We are discussing an evolutionary process begun thousands of years ago. The master intelligence of my species is still trying to perfect hybrid humans, and prepare them to assume responsibility for this planet."

As I spoke these words, I began to show signs of distress. Suddenly, I burst out of hypnosis. My eyes were staring; I was in shock, trembling, and making strange sounds, as if in pain.

Barbara reacted quickly. "Jim, inhale deeply and fill your lungs with fresh air. Listen to me—close your eyes and relax. Move to your cloud and rest there." When my breathing was finally regular again, she let me rest for a few minutes.

My mind was scattered like the pieces of a jigsaw puzzle. I was struggling to figure out what had happened. I needed to talk; speaking helped me organize my thoughts. "My integrated being has many layers, or forms. My human body is a dead end; it's the lowest, least significant, form of my being.

"I seem to exist simultaneously in at least three different forms and dimensions. I started the regression in my physical body, and then perceived the body of the slender gray alien. That gray layer is just beyond the physical body—

and that's who I saw leaving my body in the first regression. Next, I saw several developmental, or evolutionary, stages of my being.

"I don't know how many layers there are between the gray alien and the entity who just spoke to you. But I can tell you that this last one is apparently the original form of my being and he's still out there somewhere, still viable. Also...he seems to be some kind of interdimensional reptile."

"You mean Old Big Head is a *reptile?*" Kyle asked. We all laughed, and I continued my description.

"He's between eight and twelve feet tall. The heels of his feet are similar to ours, but his feet are elongated. The toes aren't graduated; they're all of the same length and bone structure, and their multiple joints make his feet extremely pliable. His legs aren't like ours. He has knee joints, but his lower leg bone only has a thin covering of muscles and skin."

These were the extremities I'd glimpsed nearly two years before, and although they still felt disturbing, I now understood that this was simply an unfamiliar form of my being. "There's a web between his torso and arms, like a bat—which can sometimes make him look as if he has wings.

"His head is the shape of a watermelon, large, and elongated horizontally. Most of his skin is greenish, and rougher than human skin. His face is reddish, and his body has hues of red, green, yellow, and orange. His torso looks humanoid, but his back has a large finlike appendage, and... although I didn't see a tail, I could feel it.

"On the larger areas of his body, like his back, the skin is rougher than other areas, like the insides of the arms. His torso has patterns of pointy skin protuberances. On his arms, legs, and face, the patterns are smaller and less pronounced.

"By the way, did I mention that this species didn't originate on Earth?"

"Yes," Barbara replied. "When they arrived, did they take control of the Earth?"

"Oh, definitely. They demanded absolute supremacy. However, only a few of them were present in the earliest days here. Only a few interdimensional reptilian astronauts colonized the Earth, and they had difficulty reproducing on this planet."

"Do you know how they lived here? Or what their dwellings were like?"

"They lived in subterranean shelters. The conditions in the Earth's atmosphere threatened their survival, because they couldn't maintain a constant body temperature."

"Was the light uncomfortable for their eyes?"

"Yes, their eyes were sensitive to light but they were more concerned about temperature shifts. Temperature changes traumatize them more than light."

I wondered what technology they had brought with them and how they had adapted it to this planet. As if reading my mind, Barbara asked, "Is the whole planet networked with the large top-like objects? Did the aliens install them?"

"Yes. They're buried all over the planet, and they've been operating for a long time. They function like underground satellites—they're used for guidance and communication. I think they're some form of energy."

"Perhaps the aliens used this technology to transport you from your house to the farm," Barbara said, and reminded me of my comments about the numeric grid system.

"Yes, it's all based on a system of numbers. If I were an interdimensional being who wanted to travel to a distant location, I'd visualize the number of the nearest anchor—and in the blink of an eye, I'd be at my destination."

"Perhaps it's a transportation system that functions on waves or currents," Barbara said.

"And transforms time and matter," Kyle added.

"Yes. It seems to do all those things."

Barbara recalled my description of being abducted by alien signals. "This may be the explanation of those signals. This may be the technology they use to transport people between dimensions."

Suddenly, Barbara asked, "What should we call them now? 'Alien' means 'foreign, strange, or extraterrestrial'— and that doesn't seem appropriate anymore."

We searched for a better word. It wasn't easy, and the search for a more appropriate term required us to reconsider all our ideas about "aliens."

Finally, Kyle suggested, "Maybe we should call them IDBs…for 'interdimensional beings.'"

We laughed, and agreed it was the best term we could come up with.

Barbara said, "Jim, I was really worried when you went through all those changes. Your transformation to Old Big Head seemed quite traumatic."

"I don't remember that part of the regression at all. But I do have one lingering impression of this experience. It was like walking to a window, opening the blinds, and looking through the open window. I just had a glimpse of the interdimensional world—but I already know it better."

"We've been assuming that superior beings were trying to take over the planet," Kyle said, "but, according to Old Big Head, the opposite is really happening. Could superior beings really be trying to guide us into a new age, in which human hybrids will manage the planet?"

I replied, "The hybridization process must have started long ago. Reptilian astronauts must have experimented with modifying human bodies and improving human brains. But now they may be approaching the conclusion of their human program. Consider the rapid advances in our technology, and the increasing number of their contacts with humans. These may be signs that they're relinquishing their control."

As I said these words, piercing pain stabbed my head again. Barbara and Kyle sat silently while I gripped my head. When I was able to speak, I said, "This regression was a breakthrough. I've learned so much today that I can't express yet. Now I know who's connected to the legs that scared me so much, almost two years ago. I'm no longer afraid to look and learn. And eventually, I may be able to contact the intelligence of other layers of my being, too."

14 | RETURN OF OLD BIG HEAD

WHEN KYLE and I arrived at Barbara's the next morning, Jane was already there. "Good news. Her morning sickness has ended," Barbara said as we came in. "And we have lots to talk about today." As we got settled on the sofa, she said, "Jim, I'd like you and Jane to sit next to each other, so I can interview you together." As I watched Barbara fuss with her recording equipment, I recognized the familiar clues that she had something important to share. Jane, Kyle, and I waited like attentive school children for their teacher's instructions.

Finally she was ready to start.

"Five people reported blue liquid or blue powder episodes in their dreams or encounters this week. You were the first, Jim; you reported being in a pool of blue liquid. What's the connection?"

I was stunned. I couldn't think clearly. I asked Barbara who the other four people were—and saw by Jane's reaction that she must have been one of them.

Barbara generally maintains strict confidentiality, so I don't know why I thought she would reveal the other names. But in this case, I knew the others and had discussed their earlier encounters with them, so she was willing to tell me. When I heard the names, I understood why Barbara was so excited.

All four of these people had reported seeing my image during an encounter—and all of these encounters had included sexual experiences with my image. Yet most of these encounters had occurred before I'd even met the person involved. "What's the connection…" I repeated.

"Go ahead, Jim."

The idea of five people having similar, and possibly related, interdimensional experiences in one week left me speechless. One of my earlier comments to Barbara came back to haunt me. In a moment of confidence, I'd said, "If you can ask the right questions, I can provide the answers."

"Okay, it's showtime!" I said, trying to break the pressure I was feeling. My mind felt like a broken movie projector, trying to rewind and fast forward at the same time. I didn't have one clear image or thought. I looked at Barbara and said, "Perhaps you should hypnotize me before asking this question."

"Great idea. I'll put you into hypnosis and we'll look at your experience in the blue liquid."

Our interview now turned into another hypnosis session. I positioned myself on the familiar cloud of cushions, stretched my toes and fingers, and began to relax. Jane and Kyle settled in to observe. As we prepared for our second regression of the weekend, none of us mentioned Old Big Head—but I'm sure we were all wondering if he'd make another appearance.

Except for a gentle breeze that occasionally ruffled the curtains, the room was still and quiet. Barbara's soft voice wafted to me on waves of fresh spring air. I was feeling light and free when I heard her say, "You're there now. Please share your thoughts with us."

"The blue liquids and powders are for ceremonial purposes, but the ceremonies aren't occurring in the present time. These recent reports are the memories of ancient ceremonial events, which these individuals shared thousands of years ago." My voice trailed off, as if I were falling into a deep sleep. In a feeble voice I said, "Memories of ancient ceremonies are resurfacing in the conscious minds of certain people. We are now gathering certain individuals who participated in these ceremonies in ancient times."

"I'd like to know more about this," Barbara said.

"We are coming full circle," I said weakly. "We are assembling people who share certain beliefs about human beings, who understand the evolution of human life. Certain people are being brought together, and the purpose of this gathering is to reenact, or complete, a process they started a long time ago. The preparations are almost complete." Now my voice returned to full volume. "But two or three of the participants are not prepared yet. We must find them and bring them into our circle before we can begin the reenactment."

Then something shifted, and I couldn't speak. I seemed to be floating and gliding through space; my thoughts were scattered. I tried to gather and hold them, but they were elusive. I had impressions of ancient Egypt. *These people have returned to human life and are preparing to participate in profound experiences,* I thought. Then my thoughts darted away again, and although I soon caught up with them, I could see that they were leading me away from the conscious world. I reached out and grabbed another thought: *These people are making conscious connections with Barbara and interdimensional connections with me.*

"Can we back up? I'm lost in space. I don't know where to start."

"Please collect your thoughts," Barbara said. "You're doing a good job. You're working with a very interesting thought wave."

I started to tell Barbara what I'd seen—images of ancient Egypt and the faces of a few familiar Egyptians. "I passed through a long, narrow corridor, with walls covered in hieroglyphics. As I moved through the passageway, I tried to read them. I traveled through an ancient passageway that leads to the ethereal world. Do you know what I mean?"

"Yes."

"I've left the human dimension. I traveled through the passageway very quickly and couldn't read all the scripts. I'd not seen them for a long time, but they're among my memories of early human lives. They're prescriptions for passage rituals. I needed to see them again and refresh the memories of my learning in previous lives. Now I remember how to pass through the corridor of human life and enter the ethereal world.

"These people lived during the height, or just past the height, of Egyptian strength and dominance." As I said this, my voice and my mannerisms changed abruptly.

Barbara, Jane, and Kyle all observed my rapid transformation. Later, Kyle told me, "We recognized Old Big Head right away, and knew he was making a comeback."

With a regal voice and demeanor he said, "The essence of my being has inhabited the bodies of many human persons. My eyes have witnessed much of the evolution of humankind, and I've played significant roles in the development of human civilization. As I told you, I can trace my origins to the arrival of intelligence on this planet.

"I cannot relate all of the life cycles of my being. At the moment, however, I am in a tomb that represents one of my lifetimes. For your benefit, I am assimilating the knowledge of this human life."

"Please take your time. Tell us what we need to know."

"During this lifetime, I took the name of a crane bird and integrated its stamina and delicacy into my being. My image was preserved in beautiful artifacts. Objects were carved and cast in my image, in my honor. Most of these objects have been removed from my tomb and dispersed. I enjoy visiting them, however.

"The remains of a human body also still exist. The body is familiar, but unaccommodating, because my essence passed from it so long ago."

Old Big Head seemed to be recalling fond memories of a glorious lifetime. Then he moved to another topic. "Now I am ready to tell you something about yourselves. I am sharing this information to confirm your own thoughts and to accelerate your acceptance of yourselves and your missions. You share the intelligence of the master race. Your ancestors created human civilizations on this planet."

"Are you saying that we're human hybrids?"

"Correct. Descendants of the original intelligence pass through cyclical human gatherings, and you are living during an important time. Many beings who have lived in grand moments of your history are reconvening. By 'grand moments,' I mean times when you amassed material wealth, enjoyed prestige and power, and experienced intellectual and technological growth.

"The impending gathering will not be like earlier times of dominance and opulence, however. The beings who are convening at this time will not create monuments, establish dynasties, or develop civilizations. They are coming together to make decisions. They will discover information about their true heritage, which will be the basis for decisions about the future of your planet."

Barbara asked for more specifics.

"These statements may seem vague. You may not understand them immediately. Please allow me to explain."

Old Big Head spoke like a monarch addressing his subjects. "A nucleus of people is joining together, forming a worldwide web, in which each is a link. These people carry the history of human evolution through time. Now this information is entering their conscious minds, and they will disseminate it to the populace. This will have tremendous impact on the future of humanity.

"Within fifty years, the thinking of humankind will be reordered. Humans will have a great awakening concerning the government of their world. They will accept responsibility for the maintenance and the preservation of this planet.

"Human hybrids will recall, and disseminate, information about the evolution of human beings. This message will prepare the general populace for the time when humans will be responsible for the planet."

"How will this be accomplished?"

"Like most human changes! As they adjust their thinking, humans will experience conflict. Presently, only a few human minds consciously acknowledge the existence of the master intelligence that developed human intelligence and established human civilization. And before the transference is complete, destructive conflicts may occur among humans as they are forced to release old beliefs. However, that will represent the last gasp of human resistance to the acceptance of their true progenitors."

"I would like to understand this more clearly. Can you restate it?" Barbara asked.

"In other words, humans should not live in fear of the return of angry mythological gods. Rather, they must accept the master intelligence of our ancestors, and understand their ancient dependence on that intelligence. We are preparing humans for a great awakening. When humans accept the truth of their evolution, a new age will begin on Earth."

"What else can you tell us? We want to learn from you. This is a rare opportunity for us."

"The interdimensional race is no longer in absolute control. Our intelligence is being dispersed throughout the human populace, so no leader, or group of leaders, will be able to seize control of the entire planet. The human hybrid beings, who share the blood of humans and the intelligence of the species, will eventually manage the planet, without guidance from my species . . . I am tired. I cannot complete more thoughts."

"Please, rest. Don't attempt to speak."

Old Big Head rested for a few minutes, but he was still with us. Kyle passed a note to Barbara, asking, "What's your name?" Realizing that the session had gone far beyond a normal hypnotic regression, Barbara signaled him to go ahead and ask the question.

Old Big Head responded, "I have many names! I have been known as Tutankhamen. I have been known as Reston. I have been known as Joshua. I have been known as Ali Bar. I have been known as Shi Su. I have been known by many human names. I have spoken to your time using my former names."

"Could we use these names to contact you in the future?" Kyle asked.

"You are applying human logic. I can speak to you now from the perspective of any of my embodiments. My former names are just footprints in time, as is your current name. Once my essence leaves a human body, it has no name or anchor. For the purposes of this discussion, I located the remains of one lifetime in order to speak to you from that particular perspective. Is this clear?"

"Yes. Thank you. Very clear."

Barbara asked, "Would you clarify something, please? You said that certain people will convene and make decisions about the future of the planet. Should we assume any specific duties? Will we participate in important events? Are we to inform people of an enemy? Are we facing a dangerous entity?"

"Your enemy is ignorance! Regarding the gathering of individuals, you will recognize them. They will come and express their need to communicate. Some will perceive beyond physical consciousness; some will express themselves in conversation; and some will commit their thoughts to paper. You will recognize their need for expression. They will acquire important information during contacts with the master intelligence, and feel compelled to report their experiences. They will participate in a worldwide communications movement, and as time passes, their desire to awaken the populace will become an obsession."

"Would you like to make any other comments?"

"When I spoke of a gathering, I was not implying that you would gather in a room and discuss specific topics. I meant that people would seek your advice, and that you should encourage them to become acquainted with one another. To complete their missions, they must accept and recognize their common lineage. These people have worked together during other lives, and they are participating in the continuation of a mission. I shall bring forth within each one of them conscious memories of their interdimensional beings."

"Thank you. That's very helpful."

Barbara said, "Jane is here today, and she would like to know more about her being. Can you tell her who she really is?"

"Before we begin, please clarify the question."

Jane said, "My identity seems hidden; the real me is a mystery. Am I of pure human stock? Am I a human hybrid? Or am I a highly evolved contact guide?"

Old Big Head's voice sounded particularly regal. "May I open your mind to a memory?"

Jane nodded, and he continued. "I have referred to the Egyptian civilization. In this time, we entrusted knowledge to certain individuals who were honored above all others. They were the repositories of the integrity, the purity, and the memories of earlier times. Their brains were used as archives to preserve the knowledge of the masters who had colonized the planet—the original intelligence.

"I am humbled, I am overwhelmed, by the greatness of those pure ones. They were isolated from others, and dwelled in temples where there was only order, purity, and beauty—and thus they preserved the original knowledge, or intelligence, of our beings. We were interacting with the physical world, and understood how human life could diminish our ancient memories. We wanted the human experience, but we did not want to lose our intelligence. So we deposited our memories in the temples, while we experienced the physical and emotional joys of human life, including sexual pleasure. You, Jane, were among those who were set aside from society in this way.

"Today, computers could accomplish this purpose. In those times, we used the embodiment of beauty. Only those who exhibited the most beautiful physical forms, features, and qualities were selected for this honor. You were selected at a youthful age, before puberty, to enter isolation and embody the intelligence of our beings."

"Thank you. I'm happy to know this."

Old Big Head tried to respond to her, but my voice cracked, and he said, "I must go back now." I began to shudder and grimace. It was a turbulent transition; I shivered for several minutes. As my body relaxed, I said, "The blue pool was in the center of a temple; there were beautiful stone columns on either side of it. Only the privileged were allowed to bathe there. Only certain privileged beings even knew of it."

"Jim," Barbara said, "please relax. You're reentering this dimension now."

"I feel the pain," I said, grasping my left ear.

"Relax and release the pressure. Your fluffy white cloud is approaching."

On Barbara's count of three, I opened my eyes and looked around the room. *I'm back in the human dimension,* I thought. I didn't remember what had happened during the regression, but I had something to say. "Now I understand why people have seen me in their dreams and encounters. We've been locating and preparing certain people to come forward. We're helping them remember their interdimensional heritage and mission. It's not as bad as I thought."

I was relieved to know that the interdimensional self other people had seen was not doing evil things to them. I'd been worried about this ever since one person described me as the commander who controlled the abductions of humans by gray alien beings.

Although still in pain, I turned to Jane and said, "I've wanted to tell you about yourself for some time. Did the message feel right?"

"Oh, yes. I heard everything he said in my own mind first. And when he left our presence, he returned you to your own frequency. That transition is what causes the pain in your left ear. Our frequency here is too low for him, so he could not remain attached to you any longer. As you were speaking, I was about two or three steps ahead of you, and I got the same messages."

Even though I had a severe case of interdimensional jet lag, I was happy to be back. As usual, I didn't remember much, but I sensed that we'd gone far beyond the boundaries of human thinking. "There's more to life than we've imagined."

In this second performance, Old Big Head gave us a lot to study. This time, he'd been more helpful, understanding, and friendly than before, and I wondered if we'd contacted a higher level of his form.

15 | THINKING IT THROUGH

BARBARA SUGGESTED that we all watch the video of Old Big Head's second appearance. I remained lounging on the cushions. Even when it was over, my mind and body still didn't feel fully integrated; a few threads of my being were still clinging to the other dimension. I didn't feel ready to be human yet.

I wanted to be alone for a few minutes, so I stood up and forced my wobbly legs to move toward the bathroom. Although I'd been there so many times before, Barbara's house seemed unfamiliar. As I doused my face with cold water, I thought, *You must be in one mind and one body*. I looked into the mirror, while the water dripped from my face. "Who are you?" I asked aloud. The tired-looking face also looked unfamiliar. "You're not who you think you are, and you must accept this!" I said.

After three years, I was finally beginning to understand the significance of this message. But as I stared at my image in the mirror, I wondered whether I would ever understand "who I am."

I returned to hear Barbara say, "We should tape this conversation." I sat down next to Jane and looked into the camera lens. I really just wanted to go home, but I understood the importance of discussing the video of Old Big Head.

"Let's talk freely," Barbara began. "Don't worry about other people's reactions. This session gave us several new insights, and we should learn as much as we can from it. Jim, now that you've watched the video, what are your thoughts?"

"Well, we've spoken before about how I was created in a test tube and programmed to be an intuitionist. I now sense that the aliens had other objectives as well. After seeing this video, I'm wondering if they developed me to serve as a communications vehicle…." Suddenly I lost my train of thought; my mind went blank.

"You were talking about your creation," Barbara prompted.

"Right. The aliens may have developed me to serve in other ways, as well. Could I be an alien communications device? Could I have been programmed to discover reptilian intelligence? Based on my own experiences, I understand how important it is for us to integrate the interdimensional aspects of our being into our human selves.

"Old Big Head has inspired us to stretch our mental comfort zones and explore new thoughts about human existence. I want to understand why my image has been present during alien encounters. Until now, I've theorized that my image was part of their alien programming or past-life memories. I was especially puzzled when people saw me in an abduction before I'd met them in real life. And I wondered if I'd really done all the things that they reported to Barbara."

"Old Big Head gave us some new insights into this," Kyle noted.

"Yes. It seems that my image is being used to tell people, "Wake up, human hybrids! Accept your interdimensional identity. It's time to discover your reptilian heritage and fulfill your mission. Does this make sense?"

My next idea was something about a relationship between alien intelligence and human sexuality, but I could not process the thought. "I've lost my train of thought again," I said apologetically.

"Please continue," Barbara said, "and don't worry about your thoughts making sense. Our goal is to gain as much information as possible. We could spend the rest of our lives trying to understand what we've heard this weekend."

I said, "So many abductees report sexual interactions with their abductors. I wonder why this occurs so frequently?"

"That's an important question," Barbara said. "Do you have any ideas about why the aliens might be so sexually oriented?"

"Perhaps there's a link between the vibration, or frequency, of human sexual energy and the energy of alien intelligence. This could explain why people so often perceive aliens and their messengers in sexual roles. So many abductees report having sexual experiences. In fact, sexuality is a common theme of all alien abduction experiences. Could sexual stimulation be part of the methodology of alien intelligence?"

"You may be on to something," Barbara said.

"This all seems to have to do with the frequency or intensity of energy."

"I'm very interested in this," Jane said. "Can you tell me why I have so many interdimensional sex dreams?"

Her question triggered a response. "It's not really about sex. Your interdimensional sexual experiences represent your struggles to receive information from, and about, alien intelligence.

They were all waiting for me to elaborate further, but I couldn't. "I just know, somehow, that the energy of reptilian intelligence is similar to human sexual energy. It feels the same."

"Let's explore another important topic," Barbara suggested. "We're now thinking of aliens as reptilian beings, like Old Big Head. In addition, I've talked to many abductees who've described traumatic dreams of flesh-eating reptilian aliens. I've documented many reports of visits to underground facilities, where human bodies appeared to be processed and stored. Although the abductees didn't actually see aliens consuming human flesh, they were left with this impression. So the question is, 'Do reptilian aliens feast on humans?' Have we gained any insight into this question?"

"You know, Barbara, I arrived this weekend with the same concern," I said. "This is the most troublesome question I have about aliens and encounters. After meeting Old Big Head, I now visualize one form of my interdimensional self as a large lizard—and he says I'm linked to the head reptiles! So I want to know the truth about these supposed nourishment centers. As you know, I've been asking the aliens to show me their complete operations, including any areas where human bodies might be processed."

I fell silent, reflecting on my own experience. After my first regression, I'd cried for weeks, because I thought aliens were developing human embryos as a food source. I also thought about one of my friends who had died. Two or three months after his death, I had a very disturbing experience, although I was never sure whether it was a dream or an encounter. In it, I passed through a long, narrow, dimly lit corridor. Its dark stone walls were covered with hieroglyphics, but I moved too quickly to read them. I arrived in a cool, damp room, apparently deep within the Earth. The ceiling, the floor, and walls all appeared to be dingy concrete. Suddenly, I saw a disjoined human leg hanging on a wall hook, and became physically and emotionally ill. I recognized the leg immediately; it was my friend's. As I turned to avoid seeing it, I saw many other decapitated and disemboweled human bodies hanging from large hooks.

When this occurred, I couldn't understand why my mind or the aliens would want to create such a grotesque scene. I'd been a pallbearer at my friend's funeral, so I knew that his remains had been buried. I couldn't understand how his body could have ended up in an alien facility. At the time, I wondered: "Do aliens clone human bodies? Do humans have multiple bodies?"

"It seems that the more we search for answers about alien consumption of human bodies, the more we end up pursuing other directions," I said. "Are we being distracted from the truth? Why do so many people have such frightening experiences? This really troubles me."

"The answer is within you," Jane said calmly, "and when the time is right, it will come. They may be able to clone our bodies, or duplicate them in other dimensions, but I don't believe they can duplicate our souls. We may have been scaly creatures during previous eras; but now we're endowed with a human spirit, a human intellect, and a human soul. In my opinion, the aliens do not have souls. They may be trying to duplicate ours, but they can't."

These thoughts were comforting. I liked the idea that there was some part of my being that the aliens couldn't invade, but the basic question remained unanswered. I couldn't understand why interdimensional beings who transcend time and matter would need to take solid nourishment from our bodies. As a reminder to myself and others, I said, "Things are rarely what they seem to be during encounters. The aliens show us what they want us to see, although a totally different experience may actually be occurring. Perhaps we should ask instead what the aliens are doing or revealing when they show us such gruesome scenes."

"Can you be more specific?" Barbara asked.

"We know one thing for sure," I said. "Every abductee who's been taken to an alien nourishment center has been deeply traumatized by the sight of severed human body parts. In my own case, I was afraid to be alone for several days after that horrifying experience. Fear was the primary byproduct of the experience. I didn't want to be tortured or to end up in that place. Perhaps the aliens were using fear to control or guide me. Or maybe they were charging my emotional energies."

"Interesting observation," Barbara said.

"But in retrospect," I continued, "my perceptions of the gruesome facility forced me to see the uselessness of my human body in the alien dimension. The aliens may have been showing me that I'd have to discard my human body to experience my interdimensional self. Maybe these facilities are interdimensional salvage areas for discarded bodies, rather than alien food banks. After all, when we journey to their dimension, we don't need a physical body."

"As Jane suggested," Barbara reasoned, "we may not be ready to understand the human processing facilities yet. But we should continue to try to learn about them." Then she introduced another important topic. "As you mentioned, Jim, aliens seem to have used fear to control you during the early stages of your awakening. Can you share more about this?"

"According to my current thinking," I said, "a few extraterrestrial reptilian astronauts arrived on Earth long before human civilization developed. They conquered the primitive humans of the time, and initiated human evolution experiments. The reptilians and their technology must have caused great fear among early humans—and the reptilians may have quickly discovered that this fear could be manipulated and become an effective means of controlling us.

"Their early experiments probably resulted in a large leap in our intelligence, leading to the development of civilization. Eventually, humans began to deify certain beings, and establish formal religions around mythological figures, who were credited with superhuman powers. I think that these myths were probably based on stories of the reptilian aliens, and that extraterrestrial astronauts and their descendants have been using fear to control humans for thousands of years.

"As you well know, Barbara, after the experience I had in March 1992, I was terrified for my life, and I lived in despair for years. But eventually, I began to accept the aliens' presence, and discover my interdimensional being. Eventually, I concluded that the aliens weren't going to kill me."

"You survived those unpleasant times."

"Yes, I did, but I didn't begin to see anything positive about aliens until I discovered my own interdimensional self. Now I'm beginning to feel some respect for them. This may simply be another phase of my learning process, but my thinking has changed dramatically. Three years ago, I perceived aliens simply as perpetrators of fear and pain;

today, I see them as the master intelligence of our world—the gods that we have always deified and worshipped. I wonder, has anyone ever seen the face of God? Is it human, reptilian, or something else?"

Barbara smiled. "This is certainly a quantum leap in your thinking—and you're still leading us toward new perspectives about aliens. You know, I recently saw a photograph of a Sumerian statue in a book on ancient art; it depicted a regal reptilian figure. There's some evidence to support your theories about reptilian astronauts.

"Also, reptiles were important in the ancient Egyptian civilization. In fact, I'm beginning to see how reptilians could have been linked to the development of all the ancient cultures."

"I'm not as dedicated to research as you are, Barbara. But I do feel a mission to lead people to answers about human life. As a child, I wasn't allowed to question the Bible—but it didn't answer my questions about existence and evolution. I wanted to know where human souls came from, and where God lived. I always wanted to ask more than they would tell me."

"I'm beginning to understand how restrictive some religions are," Kyle said. "They define boundaries of our thinking."

"Ignorance is our enemy, as Old Big Head said—but most people may prefer to remain ignorant of their true heritage. Although I was forced into my own self-discovery process, I can no longer confine myself to a religious ideology. I believe that the answers about our alien heritage lie within us. But we won't start getting the right answers until we start asking the right questions."

"Today," Barbara said, "you're happy and healthy. But you weren't happy or healthy when you came for your first regression."

"You're right. My self-discovery process has been very therapeutic. We tend to fear what we can't understand; and fear causes us to think negatively. To find the positive aspects of a situation, we must ask questions and clarify our thoughts. Typically, we don't allow ourselves to look for answers beyond the boundaries of our fear; and most fear is a matter of misunderstanding or misperception."

"You've managed to overcome your fear of aliens," Barbara said.

"After listening to Old Big Head this weekend, I realize how much time it's taken me just to resolve my misunderstandings about aliens. During my first contact, they told me, 'You are not who you think you are, and you must accept this.' But it took me three years to overcome my fear of them—and I had to work though that negativity before I could begin to accept my interdimensional heritage."

We all fell quiet, and I thought about my early experimental farm ideas, when I thought that evil aliens were manipulating us like research animals. I felt victimized then; but three years later, I had a new perspective on alien scientists. According to Old Big Head, they've invested thousands of years in improving human intelligence, and are actually relinquishing their control over this planet. "If that's true," I thought, "I'm ready to accept their interventions positively." Now, rather than feeling victimized, I felt privileged.

I asked the others if they, too, felt frustrated when they tried to explain ideas about aliens and interdimensionals to other people. They all nodded. I said, "Imagine how confused and frightened the rest of humanity will be when this information starts coming out!" I knew how uncomfortable I'd felt over the last three years, as my awakening challenged all of my ideas about human life.

"If people all over the world are now awakening at the same time, perhaps that's why time seems so accelerated now, and why people, communities, and nations are experiencing so much stress. According to Old Big Head, millions of us are in the beginning stage of accepting our interdimensional heritage."

Kyle added, "And as long as people don't understand aliens, they'll tend to perceive all alien encounters as negative experiences."

"Yes; imagine the collective impact of millions of people dealing with this inexplicable, 'negative' force in their lives."

I thanked Barbara for the brainstorming session; I was grateful for the opportunity to clarify some of these troubling issues. "When I made a commitment to write a book, I promised to help others understand their alien encounters. It's hard to believe now, but my first intention was to warn people about evil gray aliens who would freeze our bodies and transport us to underground facilities."

"Just think, Jim," Kyle said, "you've developed so many new theories about alien beings, that your book has practically turned into a treatise."

"Yes, the evolution of my thinking has been remarkable. My discovery process has taken me far beyond my initial ideas. Like Jane, I'm a few steps ahead of where I expected to be—and now I'm wondering what will happen next. How will my thinking change in the next year? What else will I discover?"

The four of us fell silent. Despite Jane's psychic abilities, we didn't know what the future would hold; we knew only that we would continue to accumulate more information, and that our beliefs would continue to evolve.

16 | PLAYING DEVIL'S ADVOCATE

I SAID, "If we're going to be responsible for the planet, as Old Big Head said, the next phase may be an education period. People of all races will have to become acquainted with inter-dimensional intelligence. Otherwise, imagine the world events that will ensue when millions of people experience the shock of meeting alien beings for the first time. If my awakening is indicative, we can assume that most people will pass through a fearful stage at first."

Jane agreed. "He tried to tell us this. People will have to discard most of their human beliefs before they'll be ready to accept the reptilian intelligence."

"Letting go of beliefs will be difficult for most people," Barbara said. "In many societies, people are taught to equate reptiles with evil or demons."

Kyle said, "Humans have a primal fear of reptiles. Most of us are deeply afraid of them. On the other hand, there are also some people who worship them. Could these extreme responses be based on interactions with our reptilian progenitors?"

We shared our search for truth about alien beings, exchanged flattering comments about our progress, and expressed our desire to know more about the objectives and methods of alien intelligence. I reminded them that we still didn't have any evidence to support our theories. Jane's encounter with my clean-shaven image sounded like more than coincidence, but it didn't provide firm evidence of anything.

Then I surprised everyone by saying, "You've heard Old Big Head, and we've brainstormed ideas about alien beings and their intelligence." Presumably, we've learned more about the aliens and ourselves. "Now, I have a thought for you to consider: What if I'm an infiltrator who's come into your time and space on an assignment to distract or alter your thinking? What would you do if you discovered that I'm an alien agent who has lulled you into positive-thinking complacency?"

"Yes!" Barbara said. "This is a new twist. What a great question."

"I could be infiltrating your camp, influencing your thinking, and confusing your research."

"You mean like the serpent in the Garden of Eden?" Jane asked.

"We know what happened to Eve," Barbara said. "Please don't tempt us with any apples!"

"The Garden of Eden may be mythical or metaphorical," I said. "But it's a good analogy."

"At least Eve got some knowledge," Barbara said. "But let's be serious, now."

"Okay. What if I am a decoy?"

"Well, you could be," Barbara said. "You have all the qualities of a superior being—you're handsome and intelligent, for example."

"Don't forget sexual!" I added.

Kyle couldn't resist this. "If you *are* an infiltrator, you're doing a great job. But, here's a thought: Who could say whether your information is leading us down the right path or the wrong path? How would you know if you were an infiltrator? We can't prove anything!"

This appealed to Barbara's love of game theories…and then she made another connection. "They say that the embodiment of evil is a handsome, dark-haired man with a widow's peak."

Jane and Kyle both leaned over quickly to check my hairline, but didn't discover a widow's peak.

"Many of the cases I've documented have involved widow's-peak aliens," Barbara continued. "They appear in both male and female bodies. I believe that these are forms of reptilian hybrids who live in another dimension—they seem to be a specific family. I've interviewed many people who have encountered them, and I realized some time ago that reptilian beings must be running the whole show on Earth."

As usual, Barbara was far ahead of me. She's always been careful to avoid sharing information with me that might contaminate my information, so she had never mentioned the widow's-peak aliens to me. I was surprised when she said she'd known for some time that reptilian aliens were in control of the Earth. I hadn't thought about this until old Big Head appeared. More pieces were falling into place.

"At first, the widow's-peak aliens seemed to be evil beings with very strong sexual energies. According to all reports, people had very disturbing sexual encounters with them…." She was trying to initiate further discussion about the widow's peak aliens. "Now, I wonder why so many people have been contacted by them repeatedly since infancy.

Do these people have a connection to the reptilian intelligence through the widow's-peak aliens?"

Barbara turned to Kyle and asked, "Have you met the widow's-peak people?"

"Several times," he said. "I can remember slithering around on the grass with them, as a baby."

Barbara continued. "My research indicates that the widow's-peak aliens are sexual beings. They're attracted to the vibration or frequency of sexual energies and strong emotions. They seem to prefer what we would call the 'dark side' of life." She confessed, "All my life, I've been captivated by the fantasy image of a slender, dark widow's-peak man. I must have some unconscious knowledge of him and his species. Apparently there's a connection; many people encounter widow's-peak aliens during dreams and contacts."

I started mulling over an encounter I'd had with an interdimensional man with a widow's peak two years before. I had reported the episode to Barbara, but I wasn't sure whether I met him in a lucid dream or another dimension. He had a very pronounced widow's peak, and his dark hair was combed toward the back of his head. He was handsome and young-looking, but I also remember noticing pock mocks on his face.

I met him outdoors late at night; we were standing on a sidewalk near my house. He said to me, "The town looks better than it ever has. You're doing a good job managing the city." Then, he told me to do something at the high school, but I couldn't remember what it was. I wondered if he wanted me to influence the students somehow. A year or so later, I was instrumental in organizing a world peace ceremony at that school.

My encounter with him may have been more involved than I remember—and when I reported the episode to

Barbara, I was too embarrassed to tell her everything. When I awoke, I was sexually aroused, and thought we'd shared a pleasurable sexual experience, although I had no memories of it. My feelings about him were haunting and confusing—I knew him, was attracted to him, and wanted to be with him. For the next several weeks, I expected to meet him in real life. But I never saw him again. He may have shared some knowledge with me, which I perceived as a sexual interaction.

I was just wishing that I had explored this experience under hypnosis, when Barbara spoke up again. "If we are the hybrid offspring of a reptilian race, rival species might exist in other dimensions. Conflict between dark and light has always existed. To me, human life on Earth is a gameboard, and we participate in the aliens' conflicts. Are we beginning to perceive the reptilians as intelligent and benevolent beings? Are they in conflict with other interdimensionals, like the great and wrathful gods who have controlled and punished humans since the beginning of recorded history?"

This was interesting, but my thoughts were flowing in another channel, and I had to say it before I forgot it. "I just had a flash."

"Oh, good. Tell us what you're thinking."

"The chain of command may be, from the bottom up: pure humans, human hybrids, interdimensional hybrids, and various forms of reptilian intelligence. Despite our earlier fears, the reptilian intelligence may well be benevolent and focused on preserving the Earth. The interdimensional and human hybrids are receiving intelligence from them and experiencing a process of self-acceptance and self-discovery. But what about pure humans?"

"Keep going," Barbara said.

"The interdimensional human engineers may use pure humans in their experiments, as well as hybrids. You've counseled hundreds of clients about their contacts with another intelligence; but, as we've discussed, you don't have enough information yet to identify the human hybrids conclusively."

"Correct."

"Therefore, we shouldn't assume that the evolution of human intelligence is restricted to human hybrids. Each of your clients has contributed to the growing body of information about the existence of other intelligences."

"Right. And people from many nationalities have reported contacts."

"Interdimensional scientists may be using pure humans and their hybrids as conduits for sharing their intelligence with this dimension," Kyle chimed in. "Think about the worldwide advancements in science, technology, and medicine of the last decade; compare them to the advancements of the previous century."

"They're astounding," I agreed. "Science and technology are changing the ways people around the world live, learn, play, work, etc. Human intelligence does seem to be receiving some type of infusions. I'm especially grateful that humanity is becoming more environmentally conscious and respectful of the planet."

Midmorning turned into midafternoon—we'd been talking for several hours. The positive tones of the discussions were refreshing, but I was ready for a break. "Our minds have really worked overtime today," I said.

"I still want to understand," Barbara said. "I want to know all about the alien intelligence. But more than anything, I want to be of service to humanity."

I understood. "All of us have struggled to understand the aliens who have intruded in our lives. We have all known pain, fear, and confusion, and now we're struggling with our own process of self-discovery. Each of us has a strong sense of mission, and is seeking guidance on how to complete that mission. I, too, feel a deep responsibility to assist those who are trying to discover themselves and understand their relationships with aliens."

Barbara said, "I started working with alien abductees more than ten years ago. I believed that aliens were treating humans unjustly, and I wanted to study and understand the intelligence that could abduct people right out of their homes like that. I felt indignation at the injustice, and wanted to find out how to protect people from alien intruders."

I said, "I understand, Barbara—but when we perceive injustice in alien activities we may simply be coming into conflict with ourselves. If we are, in fact, human hybrid extensions of the reptilian intelligence, then we're also part of the alien encounter phenomenon."

"Yes," she said. "If Old Big Head is speaking the truth, I'll have to revise my thinking about reptilian aliens. Otherwise, as you said, I'll be in conflict with myself."

Old Big Head had contributed so much to my self-discovery process. I would never have imagined that my journey of self-discovery would lead me to an interdimensional race of lizard beings. Nor did I ever expect to discover that an interdimensional reptilian race had controlled human life on Earth for thousands of years.

Soon it was time to leave. On the way out, I gave Barbara and Jane a big goodbye hug. Kyle was driving, and as we entered the open countryside, I sat back and noticed swollen buds on the trees and delicate shades of green shimmering on the large, flat fields. "All that new growth seems to have emerged overnight," I thought lazily. I was tired—but I, too, could feel the excitement of new growth.

I wondered how other people would react to the idea that our ancestors were large interdimensional lizards. "Most of the world isn't ready for Old Big Head yet," I said out loud. "Religions keep life simple for people; they define the acceptable boundaries of our thinking. After thousands of years of turning mythical stories into religious dogma, most of the world's population is quite comfortable with the old myths. They don't want to hear about human evolution."

"You're right," Kyle replied. "Most people are happy with their beliefs, and don't want to admit that their religions are based on myths. Humans seem to have developed a form of amnesia. They don't know who they are anymore."

"That's a great analogy, Kyle. In general, people seem to be in denial about aliens and, therefore, of their own ancestry." I imagined a bunch of reptilian aliens stepping into our dimension and announcing: "We're here to show you all our family album!"

"Kyle, just imagine how people would react if they learned that their gods and ancestors were reptiles. They're still fretting about the idea of humans evolving from apes!"

"If that happened, the world would change in a second," Kyle said. "The religious, social, economic, and political implications are beyond my comprehension."

"I may do some research before I write about Old Big Head," I said.

"What will you look for?"

"I'm not sure. Barbara mentioned an ancient Sumerian statue, and Jane referred to the Garden of Eden. I just want to browse through some books on mythology and ancient art. If this reptile business is true, the founders of early civilizations must have left some clues. If I search with this perspective in mind, I might find some interesting information."

"Good idea. I've wondered how you would incorporate Old Big Head into the book. You may need some historical information. Will anyone believe this?"

His question startled me. I suddenly felt pressured, and wondered how I could write about Old Big Head in a convincing way. "How will I convince people that he's real?" I wondered. Then, I reminded myself of my purpose for writing, "I just want to encourage people to ask their own questions."

Kyle's question helped me make an important decision. I said, "I'll write about my experiences as I perceived them, and will allow other people to form their own opinions and questions."

"That will be helpful for people who are trying to comprehend their own alien encounters."

"Yes, and maybe it will cause people to question the old divine creation myths."

17 | **REPTILIAN ORIGINS**

IN THE days after my hypnotic sessions with Old Big Head, peace crept into my being and matured as time passed. My fear of aliens vanished. After a tumultuous three years, I was living happily again. Although I hadn't learned much about my interdimensional reptilian self from Old Big Head, the experience of meeting him seemed to release the last vestiges of my religious and educational programming. He helped me discover my true identity, and I was contented. I had finally found a satisfying source of information about myself.

I continued to have contacts with aliens, but they were no longer disturbing. I was learning to trust them, and they seemed to play an active role in restoring my health and happiness and helping me write my book. I dedicated myself to learning more about them. If I were going to write about aliens, I wanted to be a clear voice for them.

I followed through with my idea of researching ancient art and mythology for clues about reptilian beings. After leafing through a few books about early civilizations, I realized that lizard beings permeate the literature, art, and mythology of most ancient cultures. When I read and studied from my new perspective, I was overwhelmed by the amount of information about them, and felt increasingly confident that reptilian astronauts colonized the Earth and initiated human civilization.

The art, myths, and stories of most ancient civilizations maintain that dragons, serpents, and lizards have long coexisted with humans, and that these beings can assume both benevolent and malevolent roles. Many statues, drawings, and carvings portray the reptiles as winged beings or gods who descended to Earth and became involved in the lives of humans.

Having studied history, civilization, and religion in college, I knew where to look for information about early civilizations. However, my education had not prepared me for the idea that reptilian astronauts might have initiated human civilization. Most of my history lessons seemed to be based on the biblical statement, "In the beginning God created the heavens and the Earth." These words always troubled me; they failed to answer my questions about the origins of human life.

As I reviewed literature of early civilizations, I soon realized that most religious teachings seemed to have evolved from a mixture of myths, legends, and human imagination. I was disappointed when I reread portions of the Old Testament; as a source of information about early civilizations, it was unconvincing. It seemed more like a selective exposition of the religious beliefs and practices of ancient Israel. I was discouraged to discover that the various parts of the Old Testament were written more than a thousand years apart. If so, how could it contain much historical truth?

However, Jane's words had also inspired me to reread the biblical account of the Garden of Eden—and when I looked at it from a reptilian-oriented perspective, my mind was ablaze with new ideas. It relates that an omnipotent, invisible god created a man in his own image, and placed him in the Garden of Eden as a caretaker. The man was told that he could eat freely from any tree, except the tree of knowledge of good and evil. According to the god, the man would die if he ate from that tree. "What was the god trying to hide?" I asked myself.

At one point, I tried substituting the reptilian masters for the invisible god of the Old Testament. I wanted to see how the passage would read if extraterrestrial reptilians controlled human life rather than an invisible god. The results were interesting. The Garden of Eden story might mean that reptilian masters improved primitive humans genetically, endowed them with greater intelligence, and enslaved them. If so, they probably used fear to control humans and prevent them from discovering information about themselves and their progenitors. When I read the story this way, I also realized with a shock that I had never questioned the ability of a serpent to converse with humans until I was nearly fifty years old.

This is only one example of how the entire Old Testament can be reinterpreted from a new perspective. Some scholars have suggested that reptilian beings should be substituted for the god who cannot be seen, and my research on this topic led me to a fascinating book, *Flying Serpents and Dragons*, by R. A. Boulay. The author feels that the wrathful god of the Old Testament may have actually been an extraterrestrial reptilian astronaut. Boulay says that, according to the Haggadah—the source of Jewish legend and tradition—when Adam and Eve ate the forbidden fruit, they lost their lustrous and horny hides. Does this symbolize the hybridization of humans and lizard aliens?

Boulay feels that the Sumerian King List is the most valuable historical document available to humankind. This remarkable document, which dates to the third millennium B.C., identifies and describes all the kings of Sumer. The Sumerian creation myth identifies the beginning of time as the moment their lizard-god ancestors descended to Earth. According to some accounts, Sumerian reptile gods established their cities on the alluvial plains of Mesopotamia, and it is these cities that are commonly considered to be the beginning of human civilization.

The existence and the accomplishments of the Sumerian reptile gods were extensively documented on cuneiform tablets, monuments, and artifacts. Someday, scholars may reconstruct the history of our earliest days by studying these Sumerian accounts of alien serpent gods.

The literature on gnosticism also intrigued me. According to Boulay, the gnostics were rivals of the early Christians, and their literature wasn't included in the Bible because their teachings were so different from the accepted versions. Gnostic beliefs were eventually put down by the early church authorities, and their texts disappeared in the second century; however, they were rediscovered in 1945. These gnostic tracts indicate the existence of serpent gods, and their version of the Garden of Eden story credits Eve with giving life to Adam and portrays the serpent as a noble and virtuous creature. These differences alone were reason enough for the early church to suppress gnosticism.

Most written accounts of the early history of humankind are camouflaged in religious and symbolic language. Boulay discusses mythologies and religions from around the globe that refer to flying serpents and dragons who descended to Earth to promote human civilization. For example, Chinese lore is ladened with mysterious references to an ancient dragon goddess named Nu Kau. Several early Chinese emperors claimed to be her descendants.

In addition, Boulay says that early Hindu texts, such as the Ramayana and the Mahabharata, actually describe sexual intercourse between early humans and the serpent gods. Similar early accounts of reptilian gods and lizard-like people can be found in Africa and Central America. For example, the creation myth of one African tribe describes how their lizard-like ancestors descended to Earth on a thread from a cobweb. Itzama, the serpent god of the Mayas of Central America, supposedly led "feathered serpents" over the sea and guided them to the Yucatan.

Through their art and literature, early humans on every continent have recorded the existence of reptilian beings. Some ancient texts suggest that these beings could appear at will as humans or reptiles. Apparently, they've been influencing human civilization since the beginning of recorded time. The ancient texts and artifacts are available for study, and many researchers have published their findings. I was unaware of this information until I was inspired to search for it. Now, I wonder why so few people are aware of the abundant evidence of our reptilian progenitors. Information about serpent gods is readily available.

Before I was abducted, I didn't want to know anything about UFOs or aliens. I remember how my friend Janet once suggested that I read some UFO literature. I said to her sternly, "Janet, don't read that stuff! How can you possibly believe it?" But the aliens forced me to discover the interdimensional aspects of myself, and I can recount each of the steps of my journey.

In June 1995, they set the stage for me to take another step. Apparently they wanted me to learn more about my interdimensional reptilian self and the impetus took the form of a lucid dream. When I awoke I immediately called Barbara and said, "We need one more regression. I must understand the meaning of this dream."

She asked me to tell her about the dream. I told her that it had taken place in a lovely old cathedral. "All of the cathedral walls were covered with tiny pieces of paper—there must have been thousands of them. On each piece of paper, a note was written. I couldn't read them all, but I know I need to understand the messages. The aliens must have placed important information in my mind."

"Barbara agreed. "We should investigate this under hypnosis and try to recover the information." We decided to meet once more at her house.

I knew from my previous regressions that I wouldn't be able to control my subconscious mind while I was in hypnosis. Before each of my sessions, I had wanted to explore specific encounters. But it seemed that once I entered hypnosis, my subconscious would take control and reveal what I needed to know, rather than what I wanted to know. So I didn't necessarily expect to explore the cathedral dream itself. It could have just been a message to submit to hypnosis one more time. But I did expect my subconscious to release new information for the book.

Kyle and I arrived at Barbara's house on a hot, sunny day. She was as happy to see us as we were to see her. She said, "The air conditioner in my house isn't working properly. Would you like to go into the guest house? We'll be cooler there."

Apparently, the videocamera wasn't functioning properly, either. It didn't record either audio or video of the first few minutes of the session. Afterward, Barbara and Kyle explained to me that I went under very quickly, and Old Big Head appeared right away.

The audio began in the middle of a sentence, with the words, "...his manuscript with me. I'm in a small cubicle."

"Stay where you are and stabilize yourself," Barbara said. "Please look around. What's your environment like?"

I was in an unfamiliar place, at a great distance from my body. "The ceiling is very low, so I lie down when I'm in here," I began. "The air pressure, the oxygen level, and everything about this place is different from my conscious world. My human body could not survive here. When I move around, I tire quickly, and I'm very cautious about making sudden movements. I've been warned to lie still while we discuss the manuscript."

Barbara was concerned. "Are you safe there?"

"I'm among friends, and I do not feel afraid."

Then, something unexpected happened. My physical tongue swelled up, as if it was being inflated. I could barely speak. "My tongue...it's quite large!"

My tongue filled my mouth; I had to stretch my jaws to accommodate it. Speaking was very difficult. My enlarged tongue darted in and out of my mouth, and I could barely contain it to form words. I tried to tell Barbara that other beings were with me in the interdimensional cubicle, but I had to abbreviate my thoughts. "They are friends. They are telling me information, which I need to share with other people. My friends do not want people to be fearful of them when they enter human homes and ask people to think." Then I managed to say with force and clarity, "The movement is on, you know!"

Barbara assured me that she understood, and she tried to comfort me. My enormous tongue was darting in and out, and I couldn't speak. She encouraged me to relax, and asked, "Why is your tongue so big? Is this the way it is in the other dimension?"

"It is part of my breathing process while I am here," I said, speaking awkwardly.

"Take a deep breath," Barbara suggested. "I want you to relax and breathe normally, as you do when you're there."

"Once before when I was talking to you I almost came to this place," I said. "But at the time my human mind was frightened, and I could not gain entrance."

Barbara encouraged me to experience the interdimensional environment. "I'm happy for you. You've wanted to go there."

"A part of me comes here often, while I am sleeping," I said, as if discussing a favorite restaurant. "I'm not afraid to be here. I know where I am."

"Are you beneath the Earth?"

"Yes. I am underground. Talking to you is difficult because I do not use a voice when I am here."

"Do you communicate telepathically in this body?"

"Normally. I do not use my mouth to communicate in this dimension."

My tongue remained swollen—by now it was extending one to two inches out of my mouth. I said with difficulty, "Having my tongue out of my mouth helps me stay cool."

"Are you cool enough now?"

"I am comfortable. I like to be very cool when I am in this dimension."

Barbara told me later that she wasn't sure where this discussion was headed. As usual, we weren't discussing the intended topic, and she didn't know how to proceed. "Can you suggest a way for me to help you speak?" she asked. "Is a spokesperson present who could articulate your thoughts for you?"

"I will have to speak for myself, but because of my tongue, I'll speak slowly."

Barbara tried to direct the discussion, saying, "We were going to talk about Jim's manuscript."

"Yes. The manuscript will have seventeen chapters," I responded slowly.

"The book will have seventeen chapters," Barbara repeated.

"I will bring information from this dimension. I can do it. The manuscript will be like a treatise. My mentors desire for humans to understand that peaceful coexistence among races is possible. However, another fifty to seventy-five years may pass before humans are fully capable of achieving world peace. My mentors are of the highest intelligence, and they understand that intelligent life on Earth will not prevail, unless all races coexist peacefully."

My tongue was dry and irritable after this long statement, and I asked Barbara if we could rest.

She agreed, and we took a break. She thanked me for taking the effort to deliver my messages. "This communication process isn't natural for you," she said with an understanding tone. She asked Kyle to bring me some water.

Kyle gently poured the water into my mouth. It was the wettest, coolest water that I'd ever tasted. I asked for more. It felt wonderful on my dry, swollen tongue. He placed a moist towel on my forehead, and I was ready to speak again.

"Please tell us about your body. Do you use your reptilian form when you're there with your friends?" Barbara asked.

"If I manifest in a visible form, my skin is very thick. I do not like to be hot, and my thick skin protects me from the heat."

"Is your cubicle deep in the Earth? Is it located near Jim's home?"

"I do not think of it as being close to any geographical location. It could be anywhere. It's in my mind, beyond the physical world. My cubicle, or chamber, is exactly large enough to accommodate my being. I come here to receive information and rest. When friends are present, my cubicle expands to accommodate them. It expands and contracts, and it's always in balance with the space required. When alone, I'm confined in a very small chamber, but space for my friends is automatically available."

Barbara returned to the topic of the manuscript. She knew that I had written the first few chapters, and she hoped to acquire material for the remaining chapters. She asked, "Have your mentors, or friends, discussed the manuscript with you? What information should be included?"

"I will assimilate information," I said, struggling to speak. "I will not refine it until the final presentation. My mission is to bring thoughts and ideas into your dimension. This writing project is an experiment, as are all interactions between humans and my race. We will study human reactions to the information in the manuscript."

My mouth was dry again, and Kyle asked if I would like more water. "Yes, please. I am dehydrating. Being in two dimensions simultaneously is challenging."

As before, the water was cool, wet, and delicious on my dry tongue. "Humans are very fortunate to have an abundance of water," I thought.

Barbara asked me to continue my discussion of the manuscript when I could speak again. I rested for a few minutes and said, "Four friends are assisting with this assignment, and when appropriate, we will relate new thoughts and ideas for seven of the remaining chapters."

"How should Jim proceed?"

"He will be guided. We may learn a new communications procedure. We should end this discussion now."

"Thank you for letting me know that we need to end the session," Barbara said. She asked Kyle to moisten my face.

This time, Barbara knew the importance of guiding my reentry into my human body. "Disconnect from the other dimension, and slowly return to your human form. Allow the air conditioner to cool you, and ask your tongue to return to its normal size. Rest and relax. You are returning to the human dimension, on June 24, 1995. Your mind and body are perfect and peaceful."

When I started to move around, Barbara suggested, "Please speak if you'd like to share more information. Your human speaking ability will return now. Tell us what we need to know."

I opened my eyes and looked around groggily, as if awakening from a nap. I stuttered when I tried to speak. My awkward tongue stumbled over the words. My first clear statement was, "I remember my space and my friends. They have entered my consciousness, and as a result of this, more information will come to me. This will be helpful as I finish the book. I'd like to replay this journey now, like a movie, and let you see what's in my mind."

"Maybe we'll be able to see it through you."

I thought about the interdimensional space that I had just visited. "My cubicle is fascinating. It's not confined to any definite space. Wherever I am, I can go to it. I don't know what this means, but it's interesting."

"Yes, it's very interesting."

"I don't have to live in any particular location."

"That's wonderful news. You can live wherever you choose and still be able to find your friends."

"I understand my other body much better now."

Barbara realized that I was still under hypnosis. She suggested, "As you relax and return to your human body, please review the last two weeks of your life." She paused before adding, "If you'd like to review a specific experience, move to it now."

"I understand the cathedral dream. The cathedral symbolizes a purified space, like my interdimensional cubicle. The notes on the walls represent the thoughts and ideas that I need to retrieve from the other dimension. This is a symbolic message instructing me to do this regression—to go to my other body and bring information into this world. Now, I have new thoughts that I'll use in the remaining chapters of the book."

"You seem to have a clearer understanding of the dream now."

"It was like a premonition of this interdimensional journey. My conscious mind had never experienced the interdimensional chamber before. Do you remember when I was afraid to enter it? I went there today and wasn't afraid." Abruptly, pain ripped through my head. "I'm having horrible pains in my ear," I said, gripping my head.

Barbara asked me to describe the pain. I replied, "Something enlarged in my head and created pressure. And like the other times, my jaw hurts, too."

I expected my head to explode. "I'll ignore the pain!" I shouted, clutching my ear, and continued to speak. "We made a major accomplishment today. I'll be able to return to my chamber and meet with my interdimensional friends when I want to work on the manuscript."

"Maybe they can help you with the writing."

"Perhaps they can, but we don't use verbal language with each other. That's why I had so much difficulty verbalizing my thoughts during this session."

Barbara suggested that I rest until the pain subsided. Then she added, "Let's discuss your reptilian body, if you can speak comfortably. Could you draw a verbal picture of it? Kyle and I would like to know what you look like."

"To visualize my other head, you'd have to squeeze my face until it was really long." I indicated the length and width of my head with my hands. "And my neck is very long, compared to my human neck."

"Can you describe your eyes? Are they rounded or slanted?"

"I have round eyes," I said, in a childish voice now. "My eyes are round and deep in my face." I pushed on my physical eyes. "My other eyes are deeper," I said, continuing to push my eyes in.

I was determined to show Barbara the position of my reptilian eyes, set deep in their sockets. But my efforts to rearrange my eyes alarmed Barbara. She quickly distracted me by asking about my other features.

My gestures were playful and childish. I ran my fingers through my hair and said, "I don't have any of this, and I do not have ears."

"No ears! How do you hear?"

"With my brain, of course. Intelligent beings do not rely on sound to communicate."

"Do you have a sense of smell?"

I couldn't find the right words to answer her question. "My interdimensional space is like a climate-controlled zone. Smells and impurities do not exist there."

My constant hand gestures caused Barbara to ask, "What do your hands look like?"

I displayed my human hands, while Barbara filmed them up close. Feeling the tips of each finger, I said, "You call these claws, but I don't use that word. I have nails, but they are long, pointed, and solid."

"Can you use your hands as humans do? Do you use your hands to work?"

I sounded disgusted. "You must remember—my race is intelligent. We don't do physical work. Like our cubicles, we can be nonphysical, or we can take a form. I can choose to project any body that we are discussing. But I usually prefer to exist in the form of thought alone."

Kyle asked if I had a name. I said that names weren't necessary in the other dimension. "We communicate with our minds," I reminded him.

Barbara saved the best question for last. "Do you have sexual desires?"

I told her emphatically that I did not have sexual desires. "I am intelligence!" I repeated. "How can I explain my being to you? Electricity may be the best analogy. You understand the properties and powers of electricity, but you cannot see it. In my natural state, I flow as electricity flows, and I am invisible to human eyes, unless I choose to take a form. I am an experimental being, and I am here to facilitate the removal of barriers between the physical…."

I couldn't complete the sentence. The left side of my head was again filled with devastating pain.

"Perhaps we were too close to sensitive information."

I nodded. My body was distressed and trembling. "I'll say it anyway. I would rather go back to…." Again, I couldn't complete the thought.

"Your tongue is swelling again!" Barbara shouted. "Are you returning to your interdimensional body?"

I couldn't speak. My tongue inflated immediately and extended from my mouth. The pain was excruciating; for a moment, I thought my head had exploded.

Barbara tried to get a verbal response from me. "Are you demonstrating how you can change bodies?" she asked.

In spite of my swollen tongue, I managed to say, "One of my purposes for being in human life is to remove the blockages in…"

The pain intensified, making it impossible to say more.

Barbara guessed what I was going to say. "The blockages in the minds of humans?" Then I heard her whisper gently, "Just rest."

I did rest—it was like deep, deep sleep. When I opened my eyes and looked around, I said, "I'm confused."

Barbara instructed me to relax and disconnect myself from the other dimension. "Return to the body of Jim Walden now."

"I must remember this," I insisted. "I need to remember everything that was said."

Barbara suggested, "You will have complete recall. You will remember every detail of our discussion. How do you feel?"

"Rested."

"Good. Please, come to June 24, 1995. Return to the peace and quiet of your hypnotic cloud." She gave me several suggestions to guide me into my physical mind and body before she counted me out of the hypnotic state.

"My ears are sore." I was still feeling some residual pain.

"Hello," Kyle said. "Welcome home."

Barbara seemed delighted to have me back; she said, "Please, Jim, tell us about this experience."

"Well, I know how to go to the other dimension now. My conscious mind doesn't know what it looks like, nor does it have a direction or a bearing. I can go there again, if necessary.…But I'd sure like that pain to go away," I said, rubbing the side of my head.

"Barbara, we just did something extraordinary. What we accomplished is far beyond the first flight over the Atlantic Ocean. Most humans can't even imagine doing what we just did."

"You mastered dual existence," Barbara said.

"How does your tongue feel?" Kyle asked.

I wondered why he was asking about my tongue. "It's fine."

Barbara started. "Oh, my gosh! It's normal again. Do you know what we're talking about? Stick your tongue out!"

Kyle said, "You don't know what we're talking about, do you? You'll have to watch the video."

"Jim, please stick your tongue out again," Barbara said, holding the camera for a close-up.

I laughed. Why in the world did she want to record the sight of my tongue? The expression on her face was dead serious, however. She really wanted to film my tongue. I stuck it out obediently, but I was pretty embarrassed about the whole thing. Turning to Kyle, I asked, "Is she kidding me?"

Kyle shook his head.

I mused, "I don't understand why sounds are so necessary for human communication. By the way, how long was I under?"

"An hour and a half," Kyle sighed, indicating that he and Barbara had shared an intense experience. He gave me a summary of what had happened and his report amazed me. I didn't recall most of the session, and would have guessed that I'd been under for only ten or fifteen minutes.

"I wanted to talk about specific information for the book. But instead, I gained many new insights about myself and about the aliens. My book and my mission are just a small part of the alien research program."

"Yes," Barbara said. "We're just beginning to comprehend the vast scope of our relationships with alien intelligence. And so many people are still reporting hurtful encounters with alien beings. You seem to be past that stage." She paused and said, "You're not a typical abductee. I'm very proud of your progress."

I thanked her for the encouragement, and she replied, "When I met you, Jim, I had a very hard-nosed opinion of reptilians. Because so many people have been traumatized by them, I perceived all reptilian aliens as reprehensible beings."

I agreed. "At the beginning of my alien odyssey, I perceived their intrusions as malevolent actions, too. Now, however, I'm inclined to think of the reptilian aliens in a much more positive light. I can accept them as intelligent and benevolent scientists who are researching every aspect of human life and evolution."

Epilogue | THEY ARE US

PERHAPS THE most significant event in my alien odyssey occurred on a cold winter evening in January 1995. It was one of those dark winter evenings when the sky threatens to snow, and the house was warm and cozy. My day at the office had been hectic, and I was tired; but Kyle and I were determined to work on the manuscript. We'd spent many other evenings transcribing tapes of my regressions and phone conversations with Barbara. It was tedious work, but these verbatim transcripts were essential to my writing process.

Kyle was transcribing the tape of one of my interviews with Barbara when he turned to me and remarked, "She's made several interesting comments in this interview."

I was organizing some of my notes, deeply submerged in my own thoughts. "I wasn't listening," I said. "Please replay the last part for me." As soon as I heard Barbara's voice, I remembered the discussion.

"She's doing one of her monologues," Kyle joked.

Barbara always has a long list of questions to ask at a moment's notice—and during casual conversations, her questions may be longer than the responses. She was saying, "Alien beings are responsible for sexual abuse of children, and they're present during rapes. I've documented such cases over and over. Do they enter human bodies and feel the sexual encounters? Are we necessary for their survival? Do we have a symbiotic relationship with them? Sometimes, I think that we are beyond serving as their televisions, and that we host them inside us. They seem to experience our feelings, and thrive on our emotions and passions. I've documented their presence during birth and death. Aliens seem to be intricately involved in every aspect of human life. Usually, they aren't visible; but our eyes can't see germs, either."

As I listened to Barbara's voice, my reaction to her tone of voice and her use of certain words sent me scrambling for a pen and paper. In an instant, an obscure area of my mind opened and released its hidden treasure.

The weather forecast for the weekend included freezing rain and snow—but I was willing to assume the risk of traveling through any weather to discuss my new insights with Barbara. Kyle and I arrived at her house safely on a Saturday afternoon. This would be our last session before I compiled all our information and immersed myself in writing the remaining chapters.

As we made ourselves comfortable in Barbara's office, we could hear the intimidating sound of sleet on the roof. She was anxious to hear my comments—and, as usual, decided to record our conversation.

I read the statement she had made on the tape and tried to explain what had happened when I heard it. "I felt a peculiar sensation in my head—and suddenly, I knew the answers to your questions. You provided a mental key that fit a locked area of my brain. When the lock opened, a new thought emerged. The only words in my mind were, *They are us!* I couldn't process any other thoughts."

Barbara was listening carefully.

"I wrote the words down, because I didn't want to forget them. But I didn't stop with the first idea. I also wrote, 'We are physical, conscious extensions of our multidimensional beings. Alien beings are present with us so often because they *are* us!'

"These thoughts have permeated my thinking for the last three days; I haven't been able to think about anything else. When I related them to my contacts with aliens, I began to see how humans could be dualistic beings; we live in more than one dimension simultaneously. Then I thought about the sessions with Old Big Head—and after reviewing the information he gave us, I became convinced that we are actually a multiplicity of beings."

Barbara wasn't asking questions in her usual manner, and I felt awkward. "I'm verbalizing these thoughts for the first time. Basically, my physical, conscious being, which is sitting here and talking to you, is an extension of other beings who live in other dimensions."

"You said you related these ideas to your personal experiences?" Barbara asked.

I reminded her of my illness, when I lay in a feverish coma for nearly a week. "Most of the time, six or seven aliens remained beside my hospital bed. Some of them were not external to my being—they were multidimensional extensions of me, who were nurturing, reprogramming, and reviving my human body and mind. They were assuring the survival of my integrated being."

"Are you saying that our physical, conscious self is just one facet of a multilayered, interdimensional being?" Kyle then asked.

"I've been processing these thoughts for the last three days, and yes, that's correct. Have you ever wondered who, or what, ghosts and spirits are? Most families have a story about a spirit who appeared to a relative who was ill or dying—and such apparitions may appear in various forms and identities. Also, people talk about seeing a brilliant white light just before death. Some people believe that these manifestations are helpful spirit guides or divinely inspired forces, coming to assist our transitions out of human life."

"And how do these apparitions fit into your theory?" Kyle asked.

"These spirits may be interdimensional extensions of the person who sees them, and they may be there to prepare their human counterpart for release from the physical part of life. Or they may simply be reminders of the multiplicity of our existence. And human death may simply be the process of reintegrating ourselves with our multidimensional being, rather than an expiration."

"Most people haven't even accepted spirit entities yet," Kyle reminded me. "How can you explain that humans are extensions of multidimensional beings?"

"I can only say, 'They are us!'" I replied. But he had a point. Most people wouldn't understand my three-word explanation. I added, "This theory will disturb many people. Many people spend their lives seeking a culturally acceptable form of spirituality. I believe this quest is human-created and unattainable, and it prevents us from discovering the multiplicity of our true being."

"Those are profound thoughts," Kyle said.

"Yes. In other words, our human quest for spirituality may separate our human being from our multidimensional counterparts. That may be why most humans aren't integrated with their other selves in their temporary human lives. We should be striving for integration with our multidimensional selves, rather than trying to appease an elusive god."

"That's a brand new idea for me," Kyle said.

"These ideas are still new to me, as well," I assured him. "Initially, I perceived all aliens as inexplicable beings, external to me; I felt victimized by their superior technology and their power to control me. But these apparent conflicts were simply created by my inability to grasp my own multiplicity. If we want to understand aliens, we'll have to stop thinking of them as alien."

"Do your new ideas pertain to all humans or just certain groups?" Barbara asked.

"This 'they-are-us' idea may pertain to human hybrids only. It's likely that reptilian intelligence has influenced the evolution of all humans; but as far as I can tell, only human hybrids have received specialized programming."

Kyle said, "But if you're a human hybrid, you probably don't have much understanding of pure humans. Most of your human understanding would be based on lives as a human hybrid."

"That's a good point, Kyle. All my insights and perspectives are limited to my own experience as a human hybrid."

"Do you have a feel for the ratio of pure humans and human hybrids?"

"No. I can't estimate the ratio of human hybrids to humans. But if human hybrids are being assimilated into every culture, they may eventually outnumber humans."

"If the population balance is shifting in favor of human hybrids," Kyle reasoned, "your theories may be very timely. As we speak, thousands or even millions of human hybrids may be struggling to awaken."

"Yes, these are timely ideas. Our human need to understand alien beings has intensified. Think how aliens have been popularized in books, movies, and television programs. But I don't think we'll be able to discover the reality of alien beings as long as we have a 'them-versus-us' mentality. They are us, and we are them. I don't believe I'll never make a more profound statement about aliens. Before we can understand their existence, we must discover the truth of ours."

"Those are powerful thoughts," Barbara said. "And you're right about our growing fascination with alien beings, especially among children."

"According to my theory, our interest in aliens has escalated as more and more hybrids receive a wake-up call from their multidimensional selves," I said. "Children seem to be more accepting of interdimensional realities, while we 'older models' may have more difficulty accepting ourselves as multiple beings. The interdimensional extensions of my being contacted me hundreds of times before I stopped thinking of them as aliens. For example, the gray alien who left my body during my first regression was an interdimensional extension of myself."

After a thoughtful pause, Kyle said, "These ideas will rock many people. I've never heard them before."

"They are us!" I repeated. "Some of the aliens I met were multidimensional aspects of myself. They entered my conscious world, adjusted my body and mind, and helped me understand my role in human evolution. It's more evidence that our reptilian intelligence is attempting to integrate all the dimensions, or worlds."

"You're assimilating this information and preparing to share it with others," Kyle said. "Who knows how many people will read your book, or how your theories will change them."

"Overcoming our fear of interdimensional beings may actually be our greatest challenge, and according to my theories, most of those fears are unfounded. They result from our failure to recognize the multidimensional aspects of our being. Some aliens are actually our own counterparts, but when we perceive them as external to us, we become afraid of what we don't understand, and react with fear, anger, and pain."

"Are you saying that we must figure out how to integrate ourselves with our total being?" Kyle asked.

"I can't grasp all the implications of my comments yet. But I know that my total being has more than one interdimensional layer. I can't deny the gray alien who left my body, or Old Big Head. I don't know how many layers of my being exist, or how many dimensions they occupy. And I'll never truly understand the phenomenon of alien encounters until I integrate my human self with all my multidimensional selves.

"I can't yet tell other people how to integrate their being. But I do know that we must overcome the human programming that causes us to think of our spiritual quest as our only true objective in life. Instead of assuming that a god or gods created humans, we should instead consider that we humans may have created our gods."

"Are you referring to your ideas about the interaction between early humans and extraterrestrial astronauts?" Kyle asked.

"Yes. I believe that primitive humans perceived the extraterrestrials as wrathful gods—and that the aliens capitalized on that fear, using it to control and manipulate the humans. If so, the human spiritual quest—our desire to emulate gods—probably developed as the aliens shared their intelligence with us. But after thousands of years of alien-directed evolution, the reptilian intelligence is now dispersed throughout the human population; and the need for a spiritual quest is no longer relevant. Therefore, humans should focus on the discovery of their multidimensional beings, rather than seeking approval from omnipotent gods, whom they've never even seen."

"These new insights may be the information we've been seeking all along," Barbara said. "And I find your ideas about death especially intriguing. From this new perspective, spirit beings would be our multidimensional counterparts. I've heard many reports about spirits leaving human bodies during deaths. Now I'm wondering if interdimensional beings use our human bodies to experience various aspects of human life, such as emotions."

"Yes, that's part of the phenomenon," I said.

"So that means that multidimensional beings can enter human bodies and watch life events through human eyes," Barbara concluded.

"Imagine their reports to reptilian headquarters," Kyle said, laughing.

I asked, "Do you remember my old theories about the Earth as an alien experimental farm? Back then, I thought humans were alien-owned chattel—and now we're discussing the integration of human consciousness with multidimensional entities. We may be experimental beings; but I realize now that the reptilian human-evolution program far supersedes our simple cattle-breeding concepts. Humans are literally receiving the master intelligence."

"Do you have a prognosis for humanity?" Barbara asked.

"Yes. I believe that the ultimate goal of reptilian intelligence is to populate the Earth with integrated human hybrids. By this, I mean people with human minds and bodies, who can simultaneously manifest multidimensional reptilian intelligence."

"Going back to your 'they-are-us' theory," Kyle said, "how can we reduce our fear of aliens?"

"That may be a matter of perspective. I felt victimized by my early encounters. My human tendency was to react with emotional and physical pain. In retrospect, however, I understand that both alien scientists and my counterparts forced me to constantly move toward self-discovery. Integrating my human self with my multidimensional selves was disturbing at times, but as I moved forward, I was slowly able to release more of my humanness, including my fears and illusions about these experiences."

"That's an interesting perspective," Kyle said. "How would you describe your current relationship with the reptilian intelligence?"

"I feel like a participant in a multidimensional marathon, participating in a race to save the planet. I've accepted myself as a human hybrid, and dedicated my life to facilitating world peace and preserving the planet."

"You've certainly come full circle in your thinking, from victim to participant," Barbara said. "What advice do you have for those who are still experiencing painful alien interventions in their lives?"

"In my case, Jane recognized my suffering, and led me to you. My suggestion for abductees is to seek others who've had similar experiences. Although we may be in a different stage of self-discovery, we can still learn from one another. Sometimes I wonder how I survived my awakening. I probably would have died if I'd continued to isolate myself and to think of aliens as malevolent beings.

"Eventually, aspects of my human life were removed or altered. But in return I received health, happiness, and the freedom to discover my multidimensional lives."

"Alien encounters are beyond the understanding of most people—and we can perceive these experiences either as devastating or enlightening," Kyle remarked.

"Good point," I said, thinking about Barbara's interview with the little girl. "As we evolve, we may be able to completely bypass the disturbing phases of self-discovery that I experienced. And our acceptance of our interdimensional lives will progress much faster if we believe in self-integration rather than victimization. Future human hybrids may enter life with full consciousness of other dimensions."

"When I think of the diversity of religious thought among human beings," Barbara said thoughtfully, "I sometimes wonder how we can we help."

"Old Big Head said that fifty to seventy-five years could pass before peaceful coexistence begins on the planet—and he also said that some of us are here now to prepare the way for others. These theories about human multiplicity may be beneficial to future thinkers and researchers."

"These concepts have certainly been beneficial to you," Kyle said.

"Yes; they have opened a new world for me. When our multidimensional selves come to us, we mustn't perceive them as external beings and react with fear, anger, or pain. We must accept our human lives as extensions of beings in other forms who live in other dimensions. We would be so much happier if we could interface with these other selves. But so far, this kind of communication has not been accessible for most people. "

"In the future, will pure humans have interdimensional contacts, or just hybrids?" Barbara asked.

"Pure humans will not exist in the future!" I said sharply. "I interpret Old Big Head's remarks to mean that all humans will share the reptilian intelligence within fifty to seventy-five years. Human hybrids are the carriers of this intelligence, and their offspring will disperse it. In other words, the pure human species is dissolving, and will be replaced by human hybrids."

"Wow! This could make headlines," Kyle said. "Those are profound thoughts to digest—and I've participated in your journey. I can understand the human inclination to see alien encounters as negative events, but I feel encouraged by your theories. Some encounters with aliens may be manifestations of our struggle to achieve continuity with multidimensional beings—people interacting with their own selves."

I felt uneasy as I listened to Kyle's interpretations of my ideas. My theories were still new, and they weren't familiar and comfortable yet. "Does all of this make sense to you, Barbara?" I asked, seeking her support. "I feel alarmed when you don't ask your usual probing questions."

She said, "I don't want to interrupt you. You're expressing your theories clearly, and I just want to keep the flow going. Besides, you've answered most of my questions before I've had a chance to ask them."

"As you know, Barbara, I often feel a longing to be on the other side, and sometimes I've had difficulty reintegrating myself into human life. At times, I felt more comfortable in other dimensions. Some of the pain, anger, and conflict that people experience following encounters might be attributable to their subconscious desires to stay in contact with those other dimensions."

"Do people travel to other dimensions without any conscious awareness of their journeys?" Kyle asked.

"I'm sure of it! For more than twenty years, I served as a psychic counselor—some called me a channeler—and left my consciousness frequently. At the time, I assumed that while I was out of my body 'God' was protecting me and allowing 'Spirit' to speak through my voice. I was naive! During the regressions, I experienced other dimensions."

"You used to talk about crossing back and forth between dimensions after your encounters," Barbara said.

"Back then, I didn't understand the need to maintain the continuity of my multidimensional selves. I didn't know that parts of me were residing in other dimensions."

"So, you can't avoid contacts," Kyle said. "You can't stop yourself from having interdimensional contacts, because you're actually interfacing with yourself all the time."

"That's right. In fact, I wouldn't want to stop having contacts. Three years ago, I was waiting for the aliens to end my life tragically. Now, I feel a great sense of responsibility to live and to explain my experiences to others."

"This may be the most profound conversation of my lifetime," Kyle said.

"I feel the same way," I assured him. "Now that we've opened our minds to these ideas, we'll be talking about aliens less and discussing our multidimensional selves more."

"These ideas are intellectually stimulating, but they're also a bit scary," Kyle said. "I can't imagine how other people will react to them."

"I'll have to reconsider the events of my life in the light of these new theories," I said. "I want to determine whether they really do provide explanations for my questions about human life. They may be inadequate to explain everything, but at the moment, I have clear, unobstructed thoughts about human existence and evolution, and I never had this experience before I heard the words 'They are us!'"

Barbara seemed to understand. "You may be the person who will bridge the gap between us."

"Rather than bridging the gap, I'd like to introduce you to yourselves," I said. "People need to become acquainted with their own multiple beings."

"So many of our political and social problems would dissolve if people around the globe understood all this," Kyle said.

"I look forward to living in a happier, healthier world," I replied. "But most humans will continue to credit their existence to a supreme being. Most people will have difficulty accepting these theories, until they are prompted to begin their own searches."

I felt a twinge of sadness as our discussion drew to an end. "This could be our last brainstorming session," I said. Kyle had been right; we three were capable of producing a book about alien encounters—and so much more. I was so grateful for their unwavering support and encouragement.

I wondered what was in store for the friends I'd met on my journey—and the images began to pour in. Barbara's phone would ring soon, and she'd become involved in a new case. Kyle would follow his dream of returning to college to study computer programming. Jane would be focused on her family, but she'd continue to peer into the future to help others. And I might even relocate and start over. I was wondering which world my interdimensional son would live in, when Barbara asked, "What are you thinking of?"

"The future."

"All I know is, it'll arrive on schedule."

"Yes. For the present, I'll focus on my writing and my role as a voice for the aliens. They have expanded my knowledge of their relationships with humans and instructed me to share my theories with other people. Although my account may not answer every question we have, I can encourage people to ask their own questions and seek their own answers. That's what I hope to accomplish by describing my alien odyssey."

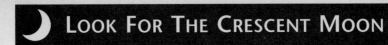

☾ LOOK FOR THE CRESCENT MOON

Llewellyn publishes hundreds of books on your favorite subjects! To get these exciting books, including the ones on the following pages, check your local bookstore or order them directly from Llewellyn.

ORDER BY PHONE

- Call toll-free within the U.S. and Canada, 1-800-THE MOON
- In Minnesota, call (612) 291-1970
- We accept VISA, MasterCard, and American Express

ORDER BY MAIL

- Send the full price of your order (MN residents add 7% sales tax) in U.S. funds, plus postage & handling to:

  Llewellyn Worldwide
  P.O. Box 64383, Dept. K779-X
  St. Paul, MN 55164–0383, U.S.A.

POSTAGE & HANDLING

(For the U.S., Canada, and Mexico)

- $4.00 for orders $15.00 and under
- $5.00 for orders over $15.00
- No charge for orders over $100.00

We ship UPS in the continental United States. We ship standard mail to P.O. boxes. Orders shipped to Alaska, Hawaii, The Virgin Islands, and Puerto Rico are sent first-class mail. Orders shipped to Canada and Mexico are sent surface mail.

International orders: Airmail—add freight equal to price of each book to the total price of order, plus $5.00 for each non-book item (audio tapes, etc.).

Surface mail—Add $1.00 per item.

Allow 4–6 weeks for delivery on all orders.
Postage and handling rates subject to change.

DISCOUNTS

We offer a 20% discount to group leaders or agents. You must order a minimum of 5 copies of the same book to get our special quantity price.

Visit our web site at www.llewellyn.com for more information.

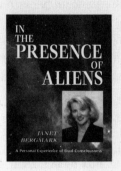

CONTACT OF THE FIFTH KIND
Philip J. Imbrogno &
Marianne Horrigan

How would the people of this country react if they knew that their government allowed an alien intelligence to abduct them and experiment on them in exchange for technological advances?

Contact of the Fifth Kind is a new approach to UFO research that is filled with hundreds of documented alien contact and abduction cases. Philip J. Imbrogno is one of the few researchers who actually goes out into the field to personally investigate the evidence. And the evidence, in some cases, is so overwhelming that even the most skeptical of readers will not be able to deny that there is an intelligence currently interacting with certain people on this planet.

1-56718-361-1, 256 pp., 5 ³/₁₆ x 8, softcover $9.95

NIGHT SIEGE
The Hudson Valley UFO Sightings
Dr. J. Allen Hynek, Philip J.
Imbrogno & Bob Pratt

In 1983, just a few miles north of New York City, hundreds of suburbanites were startled to see something hovering in the sky. They described it as a series of flashing lights that formed a "V," as big as a football field, moving slowly and silently.

It has been seen many times since then, yet the media has remained silent about it, as has the military, the FAA, and the nation's scientists. Now, in *Night Siege*, expert UFO investigators reveal the amazing evidence that cannot be denied and the more than 7,000 sightings that cannot be dismissed.

A classic in the field, *Night Siege* has been called one of the best researched and factual UFO books to date. This second edition is revised and expanded with sightings up to 1995.

1-56718-362-X, 288 pp., 5 ³/₁₆ x 8, 8-pg. photo insert $9.95

To order, call 1-800-THE MOON
Prices subject to change without notice

TIME TRAVELERS FROM OUR FUTURE
An Explanation of Alien Abduction
Dr. Bruce Goldberg

Is it possible that some of the alien abductions reported each year are actually the result of our very own species visiting us from the future (*chrononauts,* or time travelers)? In this exciting new book, Dr. Goldberg presents actual case histories from patients who, through hypnotic regressions, report strikingly similar experiences of being abducted by beings who represent us—as well as extraterrestrial futuristic aliens—from 1,000 to 3,000 years in the future. Additionally, there is evidence that time travelers have abducted the same individuals in several of their past lives for the purpose of assisting their spiritual unfoldment.

Goldberg explores the principles of quantum physics, which lend solid mathematical models to the theories of hyperspace engineering and travel through the fifth dimension. In addition, you will learn self-hypnosis techniques that you can use to learn about your own possible abductions.

1-56718-307-7, 240 pp., 6 x 9 $12.95

STRANGE BUT TRUE
From the Files of FATE Magazine
Corrine Kenner & Craig Miller

Have you had a mystical experience? You're not alone. For almost 50 years, FATE readers have been reporting their encounters with the strange and unknown. In this collection, you'll meet loved ones who return from beyond the grave ... mysterious voices warning of danger ... guardian angels ... and miraculous healings by benevolent forces. Every report is a first-hand account, complete with full details and vivid descriptions:

- *"Suddenly, a vision appeared at the foot of my bed. It was a young woman, wearing a sad expression on her strangely familiar face ..."*

- *"Running across the clearing from one thickly wooded area to the other was a thin, hunched creature, covered with light gray hair ..."*

Whether you're a true believer or a die-hard skeptic, you'll find *Strange but True* a book you can't put down.

1-56718-298-4, 256 pp., 5 3/16 x 8, softcover $9.95

To order, call 1-800-THE MOON
Prices subject to change without notice

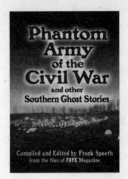

**PHANTOM ARMY
OF THE CIVIL WAR**
and other Southern Ghost Stories
Frank Spaeth, editor

A West Virginia town was named after a poltergeist and his phantom clipping shears. Read how other spirits made an extraordinary impact in Southern history and geography ...

Why did a mysterious apparition of a tall woman draped in white leave a red rose as a token of her visits? Fifty years later, the dried rose remains as evidence of her strange presence ...

Phantom Army of the Civil War features 35 stories of personal encounters with spirits throughout the South, filled with a flavor and tone that is truly and uniquely Southern. From Tennessee to Texas, and Louisiana to Virginia, these tales represent the best Southern ghost stories ever to appear in FATE Magazine during the past forty years. You will meet angry ghosts, still looking for answers as to why they are no longer alive ... phantoms roaming the countryside searching for their lost loves ... grandmothers protecting their kin from beyond the grave ... and many, many more.

1-56718-297-6, 256 pp., 5 ³/₁₆ x 8, softcover   **$9.95**